G000269726

To Mike

with love

Wynford Ellis Owen

The best is yet to come!

January 2013

x x x

NO ROOM TO LIVE

a journey from addiction to recovery

Wynford Ellis Owen

An adaptation of Wynford Ellis Owen's autobiography in
Welsh published in 2004

First published in 2010 by the

Welsh Council on Alcohol and Other Drugs

1

Copyright © 2010 Wynford Ellis Owen

Requests for information should be addressed to:

Welsh Council on Alcohol and Other Drugs,

58 Richmond Road, Cardiff CF24 3AT

Wynford Ellis Owen asserts the moral right to be identified as the
author of this work. A catalogue record for this book is available from
the British Library.

ISBN 978-0-9564985-0-2

All rights reserved. No part of this publication may be reproduced, stored in
a retrieval system, or transmitted in any form or by any means – electronic,
mechanical, photocopy, recording, or any other – except for brief quotations
in printed reviews, without the prior permission of the publisher.

Typeset in Times New Roman by
Shaun Pinney Studios www.shaunpinney.com

Printed in Wales, UK, by
Gwasg Gomer, Llandysul, Ceredigion.

CONTENTS

ACKNOWLEDGEMENTS

I'd like to thank the following for their help in preparing this book: Shaun Pinney, my valued graphic designer, for weaving his usual magic; Carwyn Evans, for his inspired images for the cover; Alun Daniel, my director, for his helpful suggestions and constant support; Amanda Lyons for her constructive comments; Rhodri Ellis Owen for instinctively knowing what works best, and Gwasg Gomer for printing the book to their usual high standards.

Thanks also to Professor David Clark in Australia, William (Bill) White in America, and Dr. David Best in Scotland, all three esteemed leaders in the recovery field, for reading the text and for sharing with me their wisdom, insight and, more importantly, their friendship.

My heartfelt thanks go to Professor Baroness Finlay of Llandaff for her kind foreword and for inspiring me to 'reach for the skies'. I'd also like to thank the Chair and Trustees of the Welsh Council on Alcohol and Other Drugs for having the courage to publish this book; members of The Living Room Cardiff Steering Committee and our Patrons, Bryn Terfel CBE, Baroness Finlay and Bryn Fôn, for their ongoing commitment to this wonderful project; and Joe and Janis Feely MBE, and their staff and clients at The Living Room Stevenage, for giving me a purpose in writing the book.

My biggest thanks are reserved for Bryan James who has made translating and adapting this book from my original autobiography in Welsh a labour of love. It has been a pleasure to work with him.

Finally, I'd like to dedicate this book to Meira, my wife, and the real heroine of the book, and Bethan and Rwth, my two darling daughters, for staying with me through all the bad times and emerging triumphant with a glint still in their eyes. Having the love of these wonderful women in my life, along with my two beautiful granddaughters, Begw Non and Efa Grug, has made the long journey bearable and, eventually, so very worthwhile. This is what I always wanted from life, to be loved. Trouble is, I didn't know I had it – until I almost lost it all.

Wynford Ellis Owen

FOREWORD

Being honest takes great courage. It is all too easy to stay hidden away in a state of denial. It is easy to keep one's shame and turmoil hidden from the rest of the world, to keep up a front. But in a world where so many people are doing this, living a lie from day to day, it takes someone with strength of conviction to realise that their story can be helpful to others and to know just why it is important to write it.

This book is just such a story. The turmoils of everyday living scream out from some pages, interspersed with colourful descriptions of some really humorous and trivial incidents. But even those seemingly innocuous events contribute to our understanding of the author's complex personality, and help us to identify with him. We see a child plagued with 'uncomfortable feelings' about himself and his relationship with others, a young lad racked with the pains of adolescence and a grown man so full of talent and energy for life, yet using his energy and intelligence to smoke and drink himself into oblivion.

At times, in Wynford's writing about his father, one can sense that stifling, intense love that we, as parents, feel for our children – a love so intense that it hurts us, the parents, and can so easily damage the child we love. How often do we say, "I just want you to be happy."? And yet our perception of happiness for the child may be far removed from the horizon that they themselves see and aim for. Little did Wynford's parents realise how tormented their child was by a fear of being unloved! But the haunting image I will keep is of the schoolboy bullied and shamed into believing that somehow, the bullying was his own fault.

More than anything else, this book reveals just how destructive alcohol can be and how influential social pressures are. It is almost as if some in society are goading others, who are vulnerable to addiction, down the slippery slope until they are trapped. Such pressures start at a far younger age than many ever admit.

Wynford describes the addictive personality, and the way external influences lead the addict to submit to the power of alcohol. It is almost as if alcohol, that simple little molecule, becomes a dictator or a blackmailer. It plays with the personality, alters perceptions and tantalisingly makes the brain blame everything else. It is as if alcohol sits there on the sidelines of life, transparent and invisible, looking on as the addict misses goal after goal after goal and gets deeper and deeper into the quagmire that their life becomes.

This book is important for parents of teenagers who are trying to understand whether their child's behaviour is normal or not, who feel disappointed at so-called failure after failure. This book is important to young people who are desperate to find another way out of their adolescent anxieties and sense of being a social misfit. It is important for the person beginning to hide behind drinking, smoking, gambling or any other addictive behaviour. This book is important, most of all, because it shows there is a way out of the quagmire. And it shows there can be life after addiction.

It takes great courage to write a book like this. It takes a comfy sofa, a warm fire and a gentle sidelight to read it, and then it takes some time to digest and reflect on the messages that this book throws up to us all. It is a good read because it is so relevant to life in our society and it offers real and durable solutions to put people back in control, or to give them the control that they never had. It shows how the damage can be repaired and leaves us with hope for the future.

The legacy of No Room to Live must be the Living Room Cardiff project.

Professor Baroness Finlay of Llandaff

PROLOGUE

Before writing my autobiography I had spent twelve years talking to people about my experiences as an alcoholic. In doing so, my hope was that I might be able to help someone, even one person, avoid the hell I'd gone through before 1992, when I stopped drinking.

When I was approached about writing a book about it, the idea appealed to me, naturally, but it took me a while to put pen to paper. There were two things holding me back. Firstly, I wanted to be able to describe 'the most perfect day' in my recovery – so I waited and waited until, in the end, I realised that by now, every day was a perfect day! Secondly, what if I were to say things that I shouldn't? Should I hold things back in case people got hurt, especially those who were near and dear to me? Those people had surely endured enough suffering already in private – without having it chronicled for posterity! After much soul searching it became clear that if my story were to be of any help to anyone, then it had to be honest, even painfully honest.

When an alcoholic sobers up it's good to have the support of another alcoholic who's been sober for a while and who has got used to dealing with day-to-day problems without the 'help' of alcohol. Such a person is known as a 'sponsor'. My sponsor was Bryn. He told me that he'd visited 33 different countries in six years at the time he was drinking, in an effort to escape from his problems. It was only after he stopped drinking that he realised that each time he moved to a different country, he was taking the problem with him – because he himself *was* the problem! Bryn died of lung cancer in 2001 at the age of 60. But during his 25 years of sober living he was a pillar of the worldwide recovery fellowship. He saved the lives of hundreds of fellow sufferers and his wisdom was widely acknowledged. His advice and support were invaluable to me in my difficult early days as a recovering alcoholic; he was like a second father to me and he loved me unconditionally to the very end.

At times I feel the need to meditate, and in my imagination I visit a heavenly garden where I meet certain people. Bryn is there, and so is Jane, a young mother who committed suicide by jumping off a bridge on Eastern Avenue near the University Hospital of Wales in Cardiff. Also Julie, who drank herself to death in a cold hovel in Riverside; Rob, whose liver exploded one night during his final binge, and Martyn, dear Martyn, who couldn't hurt anyone but himself, who died of hypothermia in a graveyard in Ely, suffering the unbearable 'aloneness' that only an alcoholic or a drug addict can comprehend – uncared for, without hope, without ... anything.

There are others in the garden, too, though not all are alcoholics or drug addicts. One of them is Graham Laker, the very able theatre producer, who died in December 2001. He is the man who helped me take that important first step towards a new, sober life. And he did it by saying exactly the right words, in exactly the right order, at exactly the right time – and I asked for help. I owe my life to Graham for that timely intervention.

In that garden, too, are my parents. I say some pretty candid things about them in this book but I've 'cleared' it with my mother in this garden. I feel that I have her consent to be perfectly honest and frank about things. That gave me courage to proceed.

1948 1955

LLANSANNAN

...one of the ladies turned on me in front of everybody, telling me to behave myself and not to be such a show-off. Nothing wrong with that, you might say! But to me, it touched a very sensitive nerve. For the first time, I became aware of a deep self-consciousness...

The first and very formative years of my life were spent at Llansannan, a small village in rural Denbighshire, North Wales, where my father was the minister of the local Methodist chapel. The Reverend Robert Owen B.A., to give him his full title.

Dad was from Dolwyddelan near Betws-y-coed, the eldest of five children. His mother died in the 1918 flu epidemic when he was only ten and his father, a quarryman and deacon, brought up the five children on his own. Uncle John became a minister of religion; Auntie Mag went to India as a missionary; Auntie Jane became a Sister in a Liverpool hospital, and Auntie Lyn, for some unknown reason, stayed at home and developed into a most vengeful and unpleasant person.

Until he was seventeen, Dad worked in the Oakley quarry in Blaenau Ffestiniog where he saw his best friend fall to his death. The shock made his hair turn grey overnight and he also became hard of hearing. He left the quarry to study at Coleg Harlech and then proceeded to the Presbyterian College at Rhyl and on to Bala College, then to Bangor and, eventually, to Aberystwyth, where he met my mother. He was a tall, studious and quiet man – except when he played football, apparently. (It's on record that in one match the whole Theological College team was sent off for foul play!)

My mother, Elizabeth Georgina Ellis, lived in Aberystwyth where she kept a guesthouse with her mother. The place was always full of students. She had one sister and two brothers. Mam was a real extrovert, and quite a stunner – a mixture of Shirley Bassey, Ruby Wax, Ginger Rogers at her most elegant, and a touch of Vivien Leigh in *Gone with the Wind*. Once seen, never forgotten! The dances at the King's Hall on Wednesday and Saturday nights were her scene, and she loved the social life of a busy seaside, student town.

How on earth Mam and Dad came together is a complete mystery! They had nothing in common; totally different backgrounds and they had such different personalities. And, in addition to all this, there was the language barrier – Mam spoke no Welsh at this time and Dad's grasp of English was, to say the least, rather limited! It was a case of 'opposites attract', I suppose!

Anyway, they got married and eventually went to live in Llansannan. That's when my mother learned to speak Welsh – out of need, really, because at that time no one in the shops in Llansannan could speak English. She learned the language as we, the children, grew up; she became fluent enough but, to my embarrassment, never mastered the mutations!

Those early years must have been a difficult time for her. How she must have longed for Aberystwyth – all the social life and the fun of the dances. Sometimes, in the privacy of our home, she would suddenly do a Charleston on the kitchen floor, do a strip-tease, or sing *We're a couple o' swells, we dine at the best hotels'*, etc. with all the actions. Moving to a quiet village like Llansannan, 'the back of beyond', as she described it, was a real shock to the system! From then on, living at the manse (the clergyman's house), she had to curb the extrovert side of her character and hide it under the bushel of other people's expectations. Unfortunately, the people of Llansannan, like most villages I suppose, had quite fixed ideas about the role of a minister's wife! As a result her vibrant personality was stifled, I'm sure of that, although she never complained, and she began to take strong sleeping tablets and laxatives. I used to hate seeing her doing that.

My sister, Rowenna, and brother, Arwel, are eight and five years older than me. The manse was known as Heulfryn, which means 'sunny hill' but that was something of a misnomer. I must have been happy at one stage, though, because I remember whistling as I roamed about the countryside – and you don't whistle unless you're happy, surely! Indeed, I had no reason not to be happy. I didn't have a care in the world (it was later that I became terribly self-conscious about my long nose) and I was allowed to play with my girlfriend, Helen, in the front garden of the house opposite us while Mam was chatting to her neighbour and best friend, Mrs. Elen Vaughan Wynne, who was also my teacher in the reception class. They were two real chatterboxes. Helen and I could have blown the world to smithereens and the two would be none the wiser! And where would Dad be? Probably fishing, or tending to his bees, or preparing his next sermon. He was an author and a poet, too, and that excused everything, it seemed. He had a right to be on his own with his private thoughts and feelings.

I was allowed to start school at the age of three. The reason was that I'd started roaming along the riverbank on my own. The manse gates were locked and barbed wire put on the boundary fences, but to no avail; I was able to escape from Heulfryn at will. About that time I remember having a heck of a row with my father. It was the village sports day and early in the afternoon Dad had won the egg and spoon race against all the other dads. I felt so proud of him. Then off he went to do what he used to do on his own, fishing or preparing a sermon or whatever, and I stayed on to play with the older boys. Soon it was suppertime, and Dad came to look for me.

"Come on then, Jac-y-do!" he said. (He used to call me 'jackdaw' whenever he was in a good mood.) "Come on Jac-y-do. Time for your supper."

"Fuck off!" I said to him. Obviously I didn't realise what I was saying, exactly, but the boys had been using this new phrase all afternoon and it had such a good, strong ring to it.

"What did you say, boy?" he replied in disbelief with his eyes almost popping out of his head.

With that, he collared me and dragged me through the village all the way home, with me crying and screaming like a pig on the way to be slaughtered. I can't remember whether Mam gave me a row as well, but I remember being sent to bed without supper with my father's words ringing in my ears.

"For goodness' sake boy, a minister's son is not supposed to use rude words like that! Now you learn that, you naughty boy, or you won't have any breakfast either!"

"But what rude words, Dad?" I sobbed. "What did I say?" But he didn't answer me. In his temper he slammed the bedroom door in my face.

That should have been the end of the matter, but oh no. He was still in a rage the next morning.

"My goodness me, boy! You will not swear in this house!"

"Ye gods!" Mam said, "What are you going to do now, Bob? My giddy aunt. Surely, Hyacinth wasn't trying to swear!"

"Nor was he trying not to, woman!"

(By the way, Hyacinth is the name my mother used to call me. No wonder I turned out the way I did!)

"I'm going to teach him a lesson, Betty – once and for all, you'll see!"

So off we went to school to see the headmaster, Mr. Teddy Vaughan. In front of the whole school I remember Dad and Mr. Vaughan spouting about 'the importance of having a pure tongue' because it was 'impossible for anything spiritual to grow in a foul mouth'. I didn't have a clue what they were on about. What I do vividly remember is that, afterwards, all the children were laughing at me and mocking me, saying that, as a minister's son, I should know better. I think it was around that time that I stopped whistling as I wandered about the countryside; obviously, there was more to being a minister's son than I had ever imagined.

I also noticed that I wasn't allowed to sleep in the religious meetings, unlike other people's children. Every Thursday evening we, the children, had to attend the meetings in the chapel vestry to listen to Dad. And, every Thursday evening, Glyn Gwynfa, Mr. and Mrs. Llew Jones's son, was allowed to rest his head on his mother's shoulder and sleep. I wanted to do the same – the meetings were so boring for young children – but my mother wouldn't let me.

"Struth! What have you got to be tired about?" she'd say, pushing my head off the fox fur that was wrapped around her neck.

Throughout my childhood, and beyond, I was not allowed to sleep during the day, or even complain of being tired. Tiredness was anathema to Mam – the sign of a weak character. The body had to be pushed to its limit all the time.

And even today, rest is the last thing to enter my head.

Another row I remember well is the one my sister gave my brother, Arwel, and me one evening. It had been one of the few occasions Arwel and I did something together. Someone had given Rowenna a pair of very grand-looking nylons as a present. Mam had gone to some practice or other. Dad had probably gone to see the chapel Treasurer – his monthly pilgrimage to beg for his wages. (The Treasurer had the unfortunate habit of forgetting to pay Dad's wages.) Anyway, that night, Rowenna had fallen asleep in front of the fire, wearing her splendid new nylons. On the wall, just below the letter rack bulging with bills and receipts, there hung a wicked-looking pair of scissors. All of a sudden, Arwel and I felt this strange urge. And without uttering a word, we both took our turn to snip the nylons. I cannot describe the thrill I felt watching the ladders zigzagging up and down her legs like the tracks of dozens of runaway trains. We knew there would be a hell of a row but, strangely, we couldn't care less. Enjoying the moment was far more important than worrying about any possible consequences.

I had a similar thrill when I set the house on fire. My father was away, preaching, and I don't remember where the other members of the family were. I was on my own, and I suddenly felt this urge. I laid some coal and balls of newspaper around the walls of the house and then poured paraffin over the lot and set them alight. What a conflagration! A passing deacon on his way to evening prayers spotted the blaze, and the manse was saved!

As a minister, my father had three guiding principles, which he adhered to very strictly – to visit his flock regularly, to preach inspiring sermons, and to exemplify the highest possible standard of behaviour in his every-day life. His sermons were always well structured and he would give his congregation some home truths without fear of hurting anyone's feelings. It was my mother who'd have to take the flack afterwards. At home after the sermon she'd often shout at him: "Ye gods, Bob! You don't give a damn what you say to these people, do you? It's me who's got to face them all afterwards! Me! Me! Me!"

Dad also had very set ideas about how a minister of religion should conduct himself. He was very critical of his brother, John, who was a minister at Llanbedr, Dyffryn Ardudwy. John had a lenient attitude towards drunkards, and would often frequent the local pub himself. Not so my father. Drinking alcohol was taboo to Dad and, in a way, it was fortunate that he had died before I started to drink seriously. To see me in that state would have broken his heart.

I don't know where these ideas about alcohol came from. Mam and Dad never drank alcohol – apart from the one glass of sherry before lunch on Christmas Day. Perhaps his prejudice against drinkers stemmed from seeing the effect of alcohol on people at the time he worked at the Oakley quarry. Certainly, there was no trace of alcoholism in his family. I was very aware of the fact that Dad, in the way he conducted himself, was trying to set me a good example – he often told me so. He did have one weakness, though – he was a heavy smoker. Although smoking is an addiction, at that time it didn't have the social stigma it has today, nor were people so aware of the health risk. So he got away with it!

As for Mam's family, it was quite a different story! They

were hardened drinkers, but she hardly ever mentioned them – especially her father. All she said about him was that he was a horrible man, nasty to her mother. I don't know whether that was due to alcohol but, knowing the signs, it was probably the case. Mam, however, never touched a drop (except the one glass of sherry on Christmas Day), and she used to ridicule people who went to pubs – 'the drunkards', as she called them. She often told me: "Don't have anything to do with them, Hyacinth. They're all bad eggs – the lot of them!"

And yet, years later, I came to realise that Mam used to take her dose of 'alcohol' in the form of strong barbiturates, and those bloody senna pod laxatives which she was so fond of. Because there is some evidence to suggest that if there is alcoholism lurking somewhere in the genes – no matter how remote the family connections – it will somehow find its way to the next generation. Perhaps not through drink, but there are other ways of 'chaining the soul'. Unfortunately, at the time, people were not aware of these other addictions, and my mother died in ignorance, without even knowing she was suffering from such an invidious illness.

When I was six years old there was an incident which was to have a profound influence on my life. The BBC came to our chapel to record *Caniadaeth y Cysegr* – a radio programme of hymn singing. Taking part in that 'festival' was an enjoyable experience, and I remember it well. But equally well I remember what happened in the vestry during one of the rehearsals for the programme. I was wearing a Roy Rogers cowboy outfit, complete with my 'six guns' with which I was going to defend the world! Being rather mischievous by nature, I was quite enthusiastic in this role-play, and I must have gone a little over the top. Suddenly, one of the ladies turned on me in front of everybody, telling me to behave myself and not to be such a show-off. Nothing wrong with that, you might say! But to me, it touched a very sensitive nerve. For the first time, I became aware of a deep self-consciousness. It felt as if a dangerous dragon, which until then had been dormant inside me, had suddenly been roused. That public humiliation, I felt, was a personal assault on me; on my own identity as Wynford. It was a 'violent emotional twist' that had the effect of causing a feeling of anger and resentment deep inside me, which was to smoulder for a long, long time.

It was still there forty years later, like a poison in my system. I just couldn't get rid of it. It was as if the dragon inside me was reminding me all the time that I was useless, that I didn't deserve to succeed and that I was deficient, somehow, as a person. That's how I had interpreted the incident in the vestry. So, I did the only thing I felt I could do – I tried to silence the dragon inside me, to ignore it and banish it to the depths of my subconsciousness. I have no doubt that this was the beginning of that cruel 'denial', which is such a characteristic of alcoholism and other addictive illnesses. "There's nothing wrong with me!" – that is their mantra. From the time of that incident in the vestry, I was filled with fear – fear of rejection, of being ostracised, of not being loved. I became afraid the dragon would be roused and that the truth about my deep self-consciousness would be revealed. That dragon had to be silenced at all cost.

One way of doing that, I thought, was to try and please people. If I could do that, then no one could criticise me; no one could say anything nasty to me, like that woman in the vestry. In my effort to 'people please' (which was another way of trying to prevent myself from being hurt again), I developed into a real hypocrite – with a false smile, a false modesty, and very cunning. I used to tell lies and deceive people; I'd use any devious means to get people to like me. But even more damaging, perhaps, was the fact that I denied to myself my true feelings.

Obviously, as a six year old, I didn't analyse what was happening to me in those terms. With hindsight, though, and with the knowledge I have today, I'm quite sure that's what happened in my subconsciousness. That incident in the vestry was a turning point in my life. Until then I had been contented and gracious; from then on (apart from a brief spell at Llanllyfni, later) I became touchy, super sensitive and easily hurt. I was hyperactive, full of nerves and anxiety. And the sad thing about it all was that I felt I had to hide these deeply painful feelings from the rest of the world. I couldn't share them with anyone.

Money, or the lack of it, was always a problem in our house. Paying all the bills was difficult on such a meagre salary as my father's. Entering the ministry, of course, was a matter of 'being called to serve' – and ministers then, as the remaining few do now, had to pay dearly for their devotion. My Dad used to say: "You become a minister either because you're serious about it or because you're a fool!" The problem was that the whole family had to suffer too. The lack of money was a serious problem and yet the community had unrealistically high expectations of the minister, and his wife, from the point of view of dress and the way they brought up their children.

Fortunately for us, Mam was a very resolute person and she was able to save money even from the most meagre of salaries. I never fathomed how she managed it. It reminded me of the story of Jesus feeding the five thousand with two fishes and five loaves of bread! But bulk buying was her secret, I think. An example, perhaps, of her excessive, compulsive nature was that she'd buy forty pounds of sugar when the price was low, and she would always buy the cheapest possible streaky bacon. Sometimes the meat was dodgy, to say the least, but each time I complained Mam would look at it, smell it, and then declare with a nonchalant air of confidence: "Struth! There's nothing wrong with this piece of meat, Hyacinth! Smells fine to me!" and then she'd cook it and eat it. Well, one day, there was 'something very wrong with this piece of meat'. She had severe food poisoning and almost died. I remember to this day the horrible sound of vomiting and retching that came from her bedroom. For some reason I couldn't understand, I was not allowed to go upstairs to see Mam in her bed. The rest of the family kept me from her. Coming so soon after the episode in the vestry, you can imagine the effect this had on me – my sense of inadequacy and insecurity was reinforced. I, Wynford, was unimportant when it came to serious matters.

The same thing happened years later when Mam had an operation in the C&A hospital in Bangor. I was the last person to be told about it, and when I asked why, the reason given was that they didn't want me to worry. But they didn't understand that I was worrying much more because I didn't know what was going on. This, again, made me think that I 'didn't count' as a member of the family – that what I thought wasn't important. This feeling – the sense of being ostracised – was playing more and more on my mind.

There's a tendency with some parents to label their children and put them in 'pigeonholes' according to their own expectations of the child. In our family, Rowenna was the organiser and the reconciler, Arwel was the academic, and I was the comedian. If there were a discussion, shall we say, on something that was important to the family, Rowenna would hold the floor. If the discussion was about politics, and politics was important in our family (Dad was a devout socialist and based his theories on true Christian values), then Arwel's views would hold sway. If I wanted to contribute to the discussion, the response would be: "Shut up, Jac-y-do, you don't know anything about it!" But if the family wanted some light relief, then it was my turn to perform.

The trouble with all this is that if you're not careful, there's a danger the child will be confined to that pigeonhole and be stereotyped, falsely sometimes, for the rest of his life. I lived in my inhibiting pigeonhole until 1994. I remember the year well because of what happened to change the relationship between Arwel and me. I was two years into my sobriety when we finally came to work together as equals in our own professions.

I'm not blaming my parents for this 'labelling' which did so much to undermine my self-confidence. I respect them and love them, now. Considering their circumstances, and in the light of what they knew and believed at the time, I'm sure my parents gave us, the children, the best upbringing possible. But throughout my childhood I had this nagging feeling of not being sufficiently loved, particularly by my mother. I just felt as if my wings were continually being clipped. On the other hand, Rowenna and Arwel had no problems during their childhood. I was the problem – the way I reacted to everyday incidents was different to other people's reaction. I just didn't see things as others saw them, somehow. The situation reminds me of a story about two boys playing happily on the beach when, suddenly, a huge wave came crashing over them. One of the boys was so frightened he ran to his mother, crying, and saying he'd never go near the sea again! The other stayed in the water, enjoying the thrill. Same wave; different reactions! Rowenna and Arwel stayed in the water – happy, contented, and brave. I'm the boy who ran away in fear – and sought comfort in any form I could find.

When I was eventually allowed to see Mam in her bed after her food poisoning, she was on the mend – thanks to the care of Dr. Thomas from Denbigh. At the time, I felt the urge to become a doctor – so that I could prevent Mam from becoming ill ever again.

By just looking at her you could tell Mam had been badly shaken. She looked pale and haggard, and was not herself for months afterwards. Throughout the whole period, I was on tenterhooks. I was worried she might die. In fact, I became obsessed with worrying about her health. I was afraid of hearing that dreadful retching noise again.

This fear began to have an effect on me. Within a few months I was unable to bear being in the same room as someone who felt sick. The fear of being sick myself, or seeing someone being sick became anathema to me for a long, long time. It developed into a phobia which blighted my life until the time I had children of my own – and then it miraculously disappeared, never to return. However, for a long period of my life this phobia was top of the list of fears that were making my life a misery. It affected my life in another way, too. I could hardly become a doctor if I was afraid of people being sick!

I remember Abel Jones, the local postman, advising me to become a surgeon – since I wouldn't see people being sick, then. It seemed a good idea at the time! Anyway, I must say more about Abel Jones. He was one of three special friends I've had in my life. (The other two were Mr. Jones the carpenter and Miss World, but I hadn't met them at this time.) Abel Jones had the fuselage of an aeroplane in his front garden, which he used to store animal feed (he had a smallholding) and to house an electric generator. Apart from the local doctor, who lived some distance away, Abel Jones was the only one in the village who had electricity – and I was able to visit him to watch the telly. It was only a small, fourteen inch set but it was the best on the market at the time. I remember watching the coronation in Abel's front room, until my dad came to drag me home. For some reason I had to go to bed early every night. And there were always threatening shadows in my bedroom. In the light of the paraffin lamp I would often see the shadow of an ugly old man with a long, crooked nose, looking down at me from the ceiling, with a weird smile. Any little noise would frighten me to death and I used to hide my head under the pillow, petrified. At every opportunity, therefore, I used to go and stay with Abel Jones at his house.

Abel had a pianola in his front room, which fronted onto

the street. On fine Sunday evenings in the summer, he would rush home from chapel, place the roll in the pianola, and then sit at it with his back to the window, pumping like mad and pretending to play the 'Hallelujah Chorus'! I don't know whether anyone was taken in by the act, but there used to be a good gathering of the chapel faithful outside the window every Sunday evening, applauding Abel Jones in appreciation of the feast of music. Sometimes, Abel would let me do the 'act', and then I, too, would go to the bay window and bow in response to the applause. I liked that sound – the sound of clapping hands – there was something special about it, and it made me feel warm inside.

The main thing about this relationship with Abel Jones was that he accepted me for what I was and allowed me to be myself – not a minister's son who had to behave himself in a certain way at all times; not a member of a family who had to conform to certain expectations – but me. He gave me his full attention, and we had lots of fun together. I'd go with him to deliver letters to the surrounding farms, and sometimes he'd let me even drive his car, his faithful Morris Minor. On one of these occasions I bumped into a gate, but Abel Jones didn't rebuke me at all. His reaction was totally different to Dad's reaction when Mam crashed our car!

Despite all her talents and ability, Mam was hopeless at driving a car – and she'd be the first to admit it! But Dad was determined that she should learn and so, we all got into BF 46, the faithful old Austin Seven, and Dad ordered Mam to drive up the hill towards Gogor Ganol. And off we went, jolting and jerking along, with the kids in the back being thrown about as if we were on the dodgems at the Marine Lake fairground in Rhyl. However, at the top of the hill, things got worse and Dad was obviously afraid for the car's well-being!

"For goodness' sake, Betty! Turn around here, before the car falls to bits."

"Ye gods, man!' said Mam, 'How am I supposed to do that?"

"Try the steering wheel!" was the sarcastic reply.

"What...?" Mam said in a confused state, "This thing?"

And with that she grabbed the steering wheel with both hands and turned sharply to the left. By pure coincidence there was a slight hump in the road at that very spot and that, combined with my mother's sharp turn, resulted in Dad's Austin Seven turning over onto its roof in the middle of the road. Dad didn't swear – he had plenty of other colourful expressions to suit the occasion! But he was in a hell of a temper as he climbed out of the car to let us out. Not even Rowenna's conciliatory powers could quell the waters on that occasion; and Mam never learned to drive, either.

Mentioning the Marine Lake has brought back memories of another thing that used to happen when I was a child. Every year, on the Llansannan annual Sunday School trip to Llandudno, Southport or Rhyl, I would get lost. I can't explain it, but I had this strange talent to disappear!

By then, Rowenna was too old to come on these trips; she was my father's darling and she stayed at home with him. So, Mam had to be in charge of Arwel and me and, inevitably, she had to take the blame for my getting lost.

"Upon my soul, Betty! Can't you go on one of these trips without losing this boy?"

"Ye gods man! Don't you blame me. Struth! It's

Hyacinth's fault – skulking off without telling me!"

"But you're his mother, woman. It's your responsibility to make sure he doesn't go skulking off, as you say."

"Rachmaninov! Look after him yourself then, man, if you think you can do any better!" And she'd leave the room in a temper, mumbling, "Ye gods! Give me a hut on the top of a mountain!"

And that's how it would be one year after the other, like a round tune. Dad blaming Mam, Mam blaming me, and no one doing anything about it.

On another occasion, my father had to visit Rhyl to attend a meeting; my mother took advantage of the opportunity to look around the shops while she was looking after me, supposedly.

Mam blamed me for what happened on that day, but this is a true account. Mam bumped into an acquaintance on the street corner; I knew that Mam was a good talker but, boy, this other lady was a good match for her! They stood there, gossiping, for ages and ages. How long can a six-year-old child be expected to stand and wait in a situation like that – ten minutes, half an hour, an hour? It felt like eternity, and it seemed to me that they intended carrying on until Judgement Day!

So, in all innocence, I wandered off and found an interesting shop window on the far end of the street. I'd swear to God that I was only there for a few seconds, but when I turned around, Mam and the other woman had disappeared. I called after her, "Mam? Mam?", but to no avail. (When she realised what had happened, she must have panicked, too, not least for fear of meeting Dad without her Hyacinth.) Anyway, after a while, I decided to walk home – and started walking towards Llansannan, 25 miles away.

I made my way to the prom and there, for some reason, I went on the open top bus that used to take holidaymakers from the prom to Winkups Camp and back. I enjoyed that trip, with my hair blowing in the wind. It was quite exciting!

In the meantime, the police were out in droves combing the streets, looking for 'a young boy, six years old, with brown hair and wearing a patterned, knitted jumper with grey, short trousers and answering to the name of Wynford or Hyacinth!' Dad's chapel colleagues were also searching high and low for me and Mam, despite being in a state of shock, had to endure the inevitable telling off from Dad.

By then I had left the open top and reached the outskirts of Abergele – on foot! And I would probably have walked all the way to Llansannan had I not been spotted by Gwilym Jones, a deacon in my father's chapel, as he drove past on his way to the dentist in Rhyl. At first glance he'd thought the little boy looked like Wynford, the minister's son, but that was impossible. He then had second thoughts and turned back – just in case! And, of course, Wynford it was.

There were celebrations in Rhyl that day, I can tell you! And for the next few days I felt as if I were the most important person in the whole world. In fact, looking back at that period in my life, perhaps that's why I did go missing so often – so that I could have some confirmation of that notion of being important (or was it of being loved?). I was never satisfied with what I had; the grass was always greener on the other side of the fence. An extra bonus on that day was that my father forgave Mam for allowing me to get lost and, after he'd made a public resolution that he, not Mam, would take me on the next Sunday School trip – just to make sure I didn't get lost ever again – we all went home in peace.

The following year the Sunday School trip went to Southport and, yes, you've guessed it! Despite Dad's greatest efforts, I went missing. The police were called out to search for me, and the coastguards too, but in the end it was my father who found me, roaming the streets, lost in my own little world. When we got back to the car park the coach had left. Dad needed his God that day, like never before. And, of course, when we got home my mother had to have her pound of flesh. "See, it wasn't me. You can't control Hyacinth either! Now say sorry, Bob, this instant!"

It took Dad a while to get over that particular Sunday School trip. As for me, all this business about getting lost was a prelude to what was to come later in life – with one basic difference: Mam and Dad would not be there to come and look for me then.

In 1955 the family moved on to Llanllyfni in the old Caernarvonshire. Whilst Rowenna and Arwel were breaking their hearts at the thought of leaving Llansannan, I was in my seventh heaven and really excited. On the day, they travelled in the old BF 46, and I went in the front of the lorry with the removal men, stopping in several pubs on the way. 'Removals' was thirsty work, they said! Seeing the inside of a pub was a new experience for me; the people and the whole atmosphere were just ... amazing! Of course, there was also the thrill of doing something I knew my parents would have disapproved of!

Almost everyone in Llansannan was sad to see us leaving

Heulfryn. The only exception was Bob Preswylfa who had put up a banner in his bedroom window declaring *'Hwrê!'* ('Hooray!')! Llansannan was a rural, agricultural community, and the Llan people were kind and generous, living life at a leisurely pace. Llanllyfni was more industrial, based on the slate quarries, and the people were more worldly, materialistic, with a more 'distant' nature. However, in retrospect, perhaps society as a whole was moving in that direction anyway.

Rowenna and Arwel would have stayed in Llansannan forever, but I was more than ready to move on to pastures new. And anyway, I had new and exciting friends and challenges waiting for me in Llanllyfni.

1955 1959

LLANLLYFNI

On the stage I became a master at
ad-libbing; I was in full control and in
my element. No one had any doubt
that acting would be my vocation.
Well, no one except my father...

lanllyfni is a fairly large village straddling the old main road between Caernarfon and Porthmadog. At the time we lived there the main employment was slate quarrying and the community was large enough to maintain three chapels and a church. At both the north and the south ends of the village there were Council house estates and these were linked by a long, narrow line of houses, some shops, a Post Office and a Police Station. This was to be the backdrop for the most exciting and liberating period of my whole life. The fears were still at the back of my mind – my mother's health and being unable to live up to the expectations of a minister's son – but there dawned a new period of adventure and freedom that I'd never experienced before.

My arrival at Llanllyfni was seen by members of the 'gang' as the coming of Christ – and they had almost the same expectations! There wasn't the 'gang culture' we have in some of our communities today; the gang was more or less the whole group of youngsters in the village, including the girls, coming together and 'doing things'. It did have a hierarchical structure, though, with a leader, a core group of five, and ten or so fringe members. The leader was Meredydd Roberts – always had been as he was the oldest, and a real bully. The first thing I did when I got to the village was to give him a damn good hiding. I did it because Linda Halliday, a member of the core group, asked me to – and, of course, I'd do anything to please. My fate was sealed as from that moment.

When I went to the local primary school I found that I was way behind in many aspects of my education. For one thing, as a seven year old, I couldn't read or do joined-up writing like the other children, and I was hopeless at sums. I couldn't concentrate in class; my mind always wandering to the slopes above the village, where my imagination knew no bounds. The one who changed everything for me was Mrs. Elen Thomas, my class teacher. For some reason she saw that I had potential and she worked hard on me day in day out, even keeping me in after school. I developed a new enthusiasm for learning and, all of a sudden, doing sums was no problem and I was rapidly catching up with the others.

The headmaster, Mr. G. R. Jones, was a wise man and he, too, had a hand in this 'revolution', always urging me on to better things. He used to give me sixpence a week for bringing him the *Daily Post* every day and the *Caernarvon & Denbigh Herald* every Thursday. I felt that he cared for me, that he wanted me to do well, but, more importantly perhaps, I felt that he liked me. I must have tested his patience to the limit because every day, yes every day, I'd forget to call for the blinkin' *Daily Post* and, after a row, I'd have to go back to the shop. The strange thing was that I didn't mind the rows and disciplining I had from him or Mrs. Thomas – they did it in such a way that they didn't disturb the dragon in me; the self-destructive ego and self consciousness lay dormant at this stage and I enjoyed the new-found freedom to express myself.

An experiment was carried out in America some years ago in which teachers were told that a certain class would have twelve pupils in it who were potential geniuses – 'spurters', as they were called, and they were expected to 'spurt' ahead of the other pupils during the coming year. The teachers were not informed who the 'spurters' were, nor were the pupils in the class aware of the experiment. The result, at the end of the year, was that *all* the pupils in the class achieved exceptionally high standards – much better than expected – with 20% achieving the highest possible marks – genius status! Only then was it revealed that the small group of 'gifted' pupils had been randomly selected and that, indeed, the term 'spurters' didn't exist at all! What was the reason, therefore, for this extraordinary result? Well, the teachers *knew* that there was a group of clever pupils in the class, but because they didn't know *who* they were they treated *all* the pupils as if they were clever. Teachers who have this attitude can change lives. Mrs. Thomas certainly changed mine.

Reading, however, remained a problem for many years – my dyslexia wasn't diagnosed until much later. For my father's generation, reading had provided an escape route from the coalmines and the quarries. He had left the quarry and worked his way through college to become a graduate. Reading, for him, had been the key that opened the door to a new life. But I had no interest in books (apart from the *Beano* and the occasional copy of *Reader's Digest*), and the constant nagging had no effect – reading, to me, was just very difficult, with the letters jumping about everywhere. I managed to hide this problem for a long time by finding a few minutes to practise beforehand whenever I had to take part in any reading exercise. The problem would only come to light if I couldn't find those few minutes. This went on for years and years. It happened once when I was a newsreader with BBC Radio Cymru (Wales); during one live broadcast a news item was put in front of me without any prior notice, and I fluffed it. I broke down completely – and that was the end of my career as a newsreader. Needless to say, my self-confidence was shattered.

Having my self-confidence undermined, however, was not a new experience for me. I well remember the occasion when Uncle John, my father's brother, and his younger son, Geraint, came to stay with us. Uncle John's wife, Myfanwy, had been suffering from a mental illness and had committed suicide. It was a tragedy that affected the whole community, not least because she had three children, Alun, Gwenda and Geraint. Geraint was about a year younger than me. At the time, unfortunately, there was still a stigma attached to mental illness, but in such circumstances my mother came into her own, organising help, comforting and offering support to everyone in need. She arranged for Geraint to come and stay with us for an indefinite period. This disturbed me immensely – not the fact that he was coming to stay with us, but that it was for an 'indefinite period'. I was a very insecure child, unsure of my parents' love. (Looking back I can see how unreasonable this was. No amount of love would have been enough for me at the time. Unbeknown to me, I was suffering from the illness of 'more' – never satisfied with what I had, and always envious of what other people had.) I saw Geraint's presence as a great threat and I was relieved when he returned to Llanbedr, because I was consumed with envy.

During that period I also developed into something of an entrepreneur, and that is how Bonso came into my life. Mr. Beeching had played havoc with the railway service and the line from Bangor to Porthmadog had been closed, making people we knew redundant and causing widespread misery. But I saw it from a different angle; to me, it opened up opportunities. The railway sleepers, seeped in coal tar, would make excellent firewood, I thought, and I could see the pounds, shillings and pence flashing before my eyes! Some initial 'market research' among friends and neighbours proved to be positive, so off I went to Pen-y-groes station to negotiate my first purchase. I had two pounds in my pocket – what remained of the 'fortune' I received in tips from the good people of Llansannan when I left – and I calculated that if I bought four sleepers at ten shillings each I could easily make £20 on my first purchase.

A kind-hearted farmer from Pen-y-groes, a village near Caernarfon, agreed to transport the sleepers home for me in exchange for a morning's help on the farm. This farmer had a dog, the ugliest black and white mongrel you could imagine. But it had beautiful big eyes and all morning, as I was cleaning out the cowshed, it stayed with me, looking at me, and I felt it was trying to tell me: "Hey! D'you want a perfect friend for life? D'you want somebody who'll never let you down? Never disappoint you? Never criticise you? I'm your dog, Winnie!" I couldn't resist it, and at the end of the morning I persuaded the farmer to give me the dog. I'd find another way of getting the sleepers home.

However, persuading my new-found friend to come home with me proved to be a more difficult task than transporting the sleepers! He seemed to have changed his mind about me and I had to drag him, squealing and snapping, all the way home to Llanllyfni. I had to show him that if he was stubborn, then so was I, even more so! When we eventually got there I put Bonso in the shed at the bottom of the garden and went into the house to announce that I was now the proud owner of a dog. Dad was in his study and Mam was in the kitchen.

"Struth!" Mam said angrily, "Who's going to feed it – this Bonso of yours?"

"Well me, of course." I replied.

"Ye gods! You watch. It'll be me, the skivvy, who'll have to look after it!"

"What's going on, Jac-y-do?" said my father as he joined us.

"I've got a dog, Dad!"

And we all trooped out to the shed at the bottom of the garden where Bonso was howling the place down. He wasn't happy at all and, as I gingerly opened the door, he squeezed through the gap and shot off in the direction of his old home. I had to walk all the way to the farm to drag him home again. I had to show this Bonso who was the boss – oh yes! After a while I ventured to show him to the gang – they all had a dog of their own – but as soon as I opened the shed door, damn it, the same thing happened again! My relationship with Bonso had a rough beginning but he eventually accepted the inevitable and we then became inseparable mates.

In the meantime I was able to get the sleepers home on the back of a three-wheeler cart that I had, and the firewood business flourished – for a while. It was greed and selfishness that brought about its demise. Each week I put fewer and fewer sticks in the bundles; the customers began to complain and the orders dried up. There was an early lesson there to be learned, but I didn't see it.

It was about this time that Auntie Mag, who was a missionary in India, came to stay with us. She was my father's younger sister, and his favourite. They would exchange letters every month. In India, as matron of a large hospital in Shillong, Auntie Mag was used to being tended upon hand

and foot, and when she arrived at our house she expected that way of life to continue! She didn't raise a finger to help Mam and when she wasn't eating she'd be out fishing with Dad, or preparing the local children for her special shows. Every time she came on her visits she would go around the local chapels and churches to show magic lantern slides of Assam. Dad would write a little play to accompany the show and she'd translate it into Hindi, for effect. These events would be quite exciting for us, the children and young people, each one learning his lines in Hindi and wearing Indian costumes, with the inevitable gravy browning to add some authenticity!

But always the best part of Auntie Mag's stay with us was the morning story sessions. I'd sneak into her bedroom, lie on the bed, and she'd enthral me with weird and wonderful tales of poisonous snakes, rapacious beasts, ... and head hunters. And all these stories contained the moral that good will always prevail over evil.

Later in the day, out with the gang in the hills and the woods, I'd re-enact these stories, maximising every aspect of romance, excitement and danger. And when the other children got tired of this role-play and went home for lunch or tea, I would stay behind in my imaginary world on top of some mountain, too 'high' to yield to such mundane needs as food and drink. Years later, at the lowest point of my addiction to alcohol, I had similar 'hallucinatory' experiences. In fact, for a period, I completely lost touch with reality. Not only did I build castles in the sky, I actually moved into them to live! I'd dream up scenes where I was the tortured hero, the victim of circumstances and other people's wrongdoing; but the hero would always emerge triumphant, saving the world from global catastrophes such as nuclear explosions, or worse, and the whole of civilisation from total destruction. Each of these scenes would end with all the world leaders coming before me in sackcloth and ashes to apologise for the cruel way they had treated me. Then all the people in the world, as one, would come to pay homage to their brave saviour and redeemer – me!

As I mentioned before, Abel Jones, the postman at Llansannan, advised me to become a surgeon, rather than a doctor, since I wouldn't then actually see people being sick. Well, as a trained medical sister, and a matron to boot, Auntie Mag was able to enlighten me as to the procedures involved in surgical operations. Needless to say, I was fascinated!

I carried out a number of experiments, on sausages and such like, but I remember one in particular – when I operated on a pork pie! It was a Friday night. Dad had been invited back to Llansannan to officiate in a wedding the next day and he and Mam would have to leave early in the morning. Rowenna and Arwel were away somewhere, and I'd be on my own all day on Saturday. So, for my lunch, Mam had bought a pork pie at the local Post Office.

Anyway, that night, after Mam and Dad had gone to bed early, I was parading in front of the living room mirror pretending to be Yuri Gagarin or Sir Lancelot Spratt, the famous surgeon in *Doctor in the House*, when I began to feel exceedingly hungry. I tip-toed into the pantry but, woe and behold, 'When I got there the cupboard was bare!' Apart from a loaf of bread, the pantry was empty – no cake, no meat, not even a lump of brawn. This was ridiculous, I thought. Then, suddenly, something interesting in the far corner caught my eye – a small basin turned upside-down on a plate. It had to be investigated and, Halleluiah, there, staring me in the face, was a delicious-looking pork pie.

I took a sharp knife from the drawer and, assuming the mantle of the famous surgeon that I was, carefully dissected the bottom section of the pie and removed the meat filling. It made a lovely sandwich! After the special treat I carefully replaced the bottom section of the pie and put it back under the basin, leaving no crumbs as telltale signs of any misdemeanour. I slept well that night.

When I got up the following day it was almost lunchtime and Mam and Dad had already left for the wedding in Llansannan. I walked into the kitchen and there, on the table, with a note beside it, was the pork pie!

'Dear Wyn,' Mam had written. 'Went to fetch the pork pie to put it in the oven, but the bottom fell out – there was NOTHING inside! I have shown it to the Post Office, where I bought it; they have phoned Robert Roberts of Portdinorwic, who made it. Someone from the company will call at two o' clock this afternoon. Be in! Mam xx.'

I didn't know what to do. All of a sudden things had been blown out of all proportion, with potentially grave consequences. There was a knock on the front door. 'Blimey! Two o' clock already! It must be him.' And whilst I dithered there was another knock, and then a third. I had no option but to open up and face the music.

"Where is it then?" said the man from Robert Roberts of Portdinorwic, as he brushed past me into the kitchen. I followed him sheepishly. He picked up the pie and inspected it suspiciously from every angle. After some humming and ha-ing, and just as I was about to confess everything, he raised his hand like a policeman on point duty and declared: 'Ah, yes ... you see! Sometimes the machine that puts the filling in the pie will miss one out. Such a tragedy when that happens! Will you accept a basketful of groceries for the inconvenience that we've caused you and your parents?'

"Thank you very much," I said, accepting his kind offer without any hesitation. Mam didn't learn the true version of the pork pie saga until she was on her deathbed. 'Ye gods!' she said, 'What other lies haven't you told me about, Hyacinth?' Well, too many, to be sure! Living a lie had become second nature to me in my futile endeavour to try and be something I was fully aware I was not – the perfect minister's son.

At the age of seven I started smoking. I used to come home from school to have my lunch – and go straight to the study to smoke the stumps in my father's ashtray. All the older boys used to smoke – and I was always drawn to emulate the older boys. I smoked tealeaves and all kinds of rubbish! By the time of the next Sunday School trip to Rhyl, I'd saved enough money from my Saturday morning shifts at Tŷ Gwyn farm to buy myself a 'roll-your-own' cigarette machine, a packet of Rizla and half an ounce of tobacco. When we got to Rhyl I made a beeline for Woolworth's to buy the necessary goods and then walked down the aisle, carefully reading the instructions. When I got to the end of the aisle, still engrossed in the instructions, I turned round and, to my horror, who was standing in front of me but my father! He'd been following me all the while. "What have you got there, Jac-y-do?" he asked, the gentle sarcasm belying his true feeling!

After that episode my father decided to give up smoking – to give me a better example. Well, that's what he told my mother and me. But we both kept on smoking just the same, on the sly – him on the riverbank as he was fishing, or at a fellow-smoker's house, and me, well, anywhere out of sight! And as time went by, I became quite a fag connoisseur! Wills Woodbines were definitely the best but they were rather expensive – one shilling and three pence for a packet of five.

Anyway, where there's a will there is a way! As luck would have it, I had started having piano lessons once a week with Dilys Griffiths at Pen-y-groes. The lessons cost half a crown (two shillings and sixpence) and the agreement was that if a pupil missed a lesson for any reason, half the fee would still have to be paid. How convenient!

The only snag was that Dilys would write a progress report in a little book after each lesson, comments like: 'A good little work by Wynford this week. But he needs to concentrate a little bit on his scales, and to practise a good little bit more each day – especially the fingering on the Minuet in G. Otherwise, a good little progress has been made.' So, it was easy peasy to copy Dilys's style – but the handwriting took about a week to master! It worked a treat for months on end, and I enjoyed my Woodbines, until Mam began to realise that the reports were not quite consistent with my progress as a pianist. I wasn't quite the budding Russ Conway that was described in the notes! Also, rather negligently, I had skipped filling in the comments in the little book for a few weeks. Truth was out – and there followed the usual ritual about disappointment and shame and being let down – but it eventually blew over. As a compromise I promised to go back to Dilys – with the aim of not being more ambitious than some tunes from the hymn book – but I didn't promise to give up cigarettes.

In addition to being an excellent teacher, Mrs. Elen Thomas was also a gifted script and music writer. Her talent in this field came to the fore one year when the school decided to take part in the Action Song competition in the Urdd National Eisteddfod*. Her choice of theme was *Barti Ddu o Gasnewy' Bach*, or Black Bart, otherwise known as Bartholomew Roberts, the colourful eighteenth century pirate from Newport in Pembrokeshire. It provided unlimited scope for both music and drama. The first I heard of it was when Mrs. Thomas asked me to sing something with her at the piano. Little did I know that it was an audition and you can imagine my feelings when it was announced to the whole school that I would play the part of Black Bart, the hero himself! Mam was in her element – her Hyacinth, at last, would be able to do something the manse family would be proud of.

There was no holding me back after that. Rehearsals were held at lunchtime and after school and I gave it my all; it filled my life; it was my cigarette from then on. All of a sudden I found that I was popular with the girls. But in fact I felt that everybody was friendly towards me – and that gave me great satisfaction, particularly the praise that came with it. If you remember, to be liked by others had been the *raison d'être* of my whole life until then – and here I was, the centre of attention and adulation! And all I had to do was to be someone else!

The Urdd is the Welsh League of Youth. The eisteddfod is a gathering where people compete against each other in activities such as singing, dancing, recitation etc..

Barti Ddu went from strength to strength, sweeping to victory at every stage of the competition including the final at the Urdd National Eisteddfod at Mold in 1958. My cup was full – and that of my parents! They were so proud of me.

On the stage I became a master at ad-libbing; I was in full control and in my element. No one had any doubt that acting would be my vocation. Well, no one except my father. He knew the value of education and his son would have to get some qualifications first.

The school took part in the same competition again the following year, with a different play and me in a supporting role, but we could only manage second place this time. I began to compete as an individual, too, doing the rounds in the various *eisteddfodau* – recitation, singing, acting – but without much notable achievement. Hard as I tried, I just couldn't recapture the glory days of *Barti Ddu*. I remember how disappointed I was. It's sad, really, when you think about it, when people fail to appreciate the good things in life just because they don't match up to the 'best' in their experience. I have a friend who saw the most amazing sunset in Acapulco in 1979 – and there's been no such sunset ever since! Perhaps not, but in denying the beauty of other sunsets he is denying himself the basic pleasure of life – to make the most of life as it unfolds and enjoy it for what it is.

Meanwhile, there were dark clouds gathering above the manse. Bonso had been seen harassing sheep. Well, that's what the farmer told us one Sunday afternoon, standing at the front door with Mr. Roberts, the local policeman, at his side. He claimed to have witnessed the incident with his own eyes, and Mr. Roberts confirmed that this was 'a very serious matter'. Indeed it was, and the matter ended up in the Magistrate's Court at Caernarfon. We could imagine the headlines in the *Daily Post* and the *Caernarvon and Denbigh Herald* – 'Minister of Religion not in control of dog!' or 'Minister's dog commits serious crime!' and, even more serious was the probability that Bonso would have to be put down. The incident was a major catastrophe for the manse family and there were long discussions as to how to cope with the adverse publicity that was bound to follow the hearing. No one listened to my pleading that Bonso could not have been the dog seen by the farmer; that he was in the shed at the bottom of the garden at the time of the incident, three miles away ... and that I had a witness. The late Ainsleigh Davies, a respected headmaster and lay preacher, was staying with us at the manse that weekend and he testified that he'd seen Bonso in the shed – but to no avail.

The night before the case was to be heard I lay in bed, restless and unable to sleep. Suddenly I felt the urge to see Bonso, to say one last goodbye, and I rushed downstairs. But Dad stopped me, saying: "Don't go to the shed, Jac-y-do. You'll only make yourself more upset." "I couldn't be more upset than I am already, Dad!" I retorted as I forced my way past him. A terrible shock was awaiting me when I got to the shed – there was no trace of Bonso anywhere!

When I got back to the house in tears my father tried to console me. "Listen, Jac-y-do," he said, his words full of guilt, "I can explain everything..." My parents had had Bonso put down earlier in the day, hoping that would reduce the expected fine and minimise the press attention. I couldn't believe my ears; I screamed the place down and accused my parents of betrayal and murder. I was heartbroken. Bonso had been my best friend, the only true friend with whom I could share every little secret and be my true self. He'd been such an important part of my life. And now he was gone, taken away from me in the most cruel way – and for no reason, because in court the next day the magistrate dismissed the case on the grounds of insufficient evidence. Needless to say, it took me a long time to get over that incident.

But, life had to go on and the rest of 1959 proved to be quite eventful. Dad had a life-changing operation on his inner ear, which improved his hearing no end. Despite suffering facial paralysis as a result of the operation, his quality of life was vastly improved. (That intricate operation in Walton Hospital in Liverpool took eight hours. Ten years later he returned to the same hospital for an operation on the other ear – and it took just an hour and a half! Such progress!) On his deathbed, when my father and I were closer than we'd ever been, he confided in me how his deafness had caused him great frustration throughout his life – not only the tension caused by having to ask for things to be repeated all the time, but also the embarrassment of misunderstanding things in meetings with the result that he'd often bark up the wrong tree and make a fool of himself. He must have suffered terribly over the years and the op was a great blessing and relief for him.

Indeed, the rest of 1959 was a very good year for the manse family. To everyone's relief, I passed the eleven plus exam (the only one in the class of four to do so), Arwel passed his O Levels and Rowenna returned home after a successful year at Barry College of Education. To crown it all, that was the year the National Eisteddfod came to Caernarfon and the organisers had invited the school to present *Barti Ddu* as part of the pageant in the opening ceremony. I gave it my all, of course, despite suffering from mumps during the rehearsal period, and it was a resounding success. There was an addition to the family, too – Sionyn, the corgi. But he was my dad's dog.

In the great wide world, Prime Minister Harold Macmillan was telling everyone: "You've never had it so good!" And people believed it. Things were certainly looking up for me. However, that joy was short-lived because in September I was to experience the entry of the Devil into my life – in the form of Mr. R. H. Pritchard-Jones, my new headmaster at Dyffryn Nantlle Secondary School.

1959 1966

HELL ON EARTH

Unbeknown to me, when I started
taking Mam's sleeping tablets,
I turned my back on the God that had
been drilled into me as a child.
I became dependent on my own
devices to find the feel-good factor.

The dragon that breathed fire inside me on that frightful rehearsal evening at the vestry in Llansannan had been silent for many years. Life had provided me with plenty of ups and downs but my development as a person had been quite, dare I say it, 'normal'. Certainly, since then, I had not heard the same evil, convincing inner voice telling me how worthless I was, how I didn't deserve to succeed and how deficient I was as an individual. Its slumber, however, was about to be disturbed.

In September 1959, I went to Dyffryn Nantlle Secondary School in Pen-y-groes, a large village a mile or so from Llanllyfni. I didn't settle there at all. In a class of over thirty pupils, I missed the individual attention I used to enjoy in the class of four at Llanllyfni. There, Mrs. Elen Thomas and the headmaster had kept my nose to the grindstone, as it were, but in this new, unfamiliar setting there was none of that individual care; everything was so impersonal. The bell was the boss and, at uncompromisingly regular intervals, everyone, teachers and pupils alike, scrambled to different lessons in different rooms. Some of us would have benefited from a little more time to come to terms with so many new subjects and concepts, but teaching and learning was just one mad rush – and, of course, dyslexia had not been discovered then!

Learning French and Latin was beyond my comprehension, and when the pupils were asked to bring bottles of wine to the French class I knew that not only did the teacher and I not speak the same language, but neither did we share the same planet! Alcohol, she obviously didn't realise, was anathema in our home. I managed to bring in some French goods but I remember being amazed at the variety of French wine and spirits the other pupils had brought in. It was obvious that I didn't live in the same world as them. Some of them said that their parents regularly drank wine with their meals – openly, in front of their children! Oh, to have such wonderfully open-minded parents, I thought! But the effect of all this was to emphasise my sense of aloneness in the world. I felt as if I was outside the classroom looking in through the window, seeing everything, hearing everything, but not being a part of it. It was like being detached from reality, somehow.

I made a gallant effort to master Latin, realising it was an essential subject if I was to proceed to medical college, as was my declared ambition. But despite Mr. John Gill's brilliance as a teacher (and he was also an excellent cricketer and footballer), his talents were wasted on me. After Form 3, I gave it up, and with it went my long-held aspiration to become a famous surgeon. And, in accepting the reality that I wasn't good enough to be a surgeon, my already dented self-confidence took another blow.

Edgar Williams the Post Office (a former minister of religion who had seen the light and become a shopkeeper) was clearing out his store one day and amongst the castaways were three bottles of brown ale. I was mesmerised, somehow, by these three bottles. I saved them from the tip and for days on end I spent some time just tenderly running my hands over these bottles, gently prizing open the caps, enjoying the rich aroma of the ale – but I didn't taste their 'forbidden fruit'. I made a secret vow, though, that as soon as I was set free from what I perceived to be this puritanical upbringing, I would abstain no more. I relished the prospect. I had an innate feeling that this stuff had magical qualities and that we were destined to be together one day. I felt it promised me so much, somehow.

When I went to the secondary school I became separated from my three friends from Llanllyfni primary school. They had been allocated to the lower forms – branded as failures by the 11+ results. I made new friends, but they were from other villages and, back at Llanllyfni, for some reason, I grew apart from my old friends. All of a sudden we had very little in common, and I began to feel lonely and isolated after school. On top of that, Mr. Jones the Carpenter, my best friend, moved to live in Liverpool. I used to spend most of my free time at his workshop, admiring his skills and marvelling at his stories, especially the ones about putting corpses in coffins. We lost touch after that, apart from a few visits during school holidays.

And that is when Miss World entered my life! Her real name was Mrs. Jini Griffiths and she was an elderly lady living in our street. She'd been widowed at a young age and had lived on her own ever since. She had very little hair but what she had left she kept in two pink curlers on the top of her head, protected by a hairnet. She was a real character. But she was also an angel if ever there was one. We became really close friends. Looking back I think how kind God was to me at that time, because had it not been for Miss World I would surely have done something silly to myself. I would visit her last thing every night and she'd be there, kettle on the boil, waiting for our cup of tea and a chat.

Then we'd go to the piano for a singsong, hymns mostly,

and I'm sure we upset some of her neighbours because this went on, sometimes, till the small hours of the morning – and she had a strong contralto voice. We had long, serious chats about everything and nothing in particular. She was quite open-minded and I could confide in her completely – well, almost. I had some shameful secrets that I couldn't share even with her. Anyway, these sessions with Miss World were important to me, as I was able to get things off my chest, as it were, with a sympathetic listener; it allowed me to balance my thoughts and re-establish my fragile self-esteem.

At this stage of my life I experienced physical bullying. Not so much during school hours, but on the way out of school to catch the bus home from Pen-y-groes. A gang of boys from the local Council estate would lay in wait for me every day and the thought of catching the bus home would be a daily nightmare. They'd tear my clothes, throw my books into the road and sometimes prevent me from boarding the bus, especially on rainy days. I didn't report it to anyone. I was afraid of the consequences, afraid the bullying would get worse, afraid of being seen as a softie. I was afraid, too, of my parents' reaction because being a minister's son was the main gist of the taunts. At the time, bullying was not given the attention it deservedly gets today. But it was as true then as it is now that the bullied person, somehow, always feels a certain guilt – as if it's his or her own fault! Now and again, when the bullies were not waiting for me at the end of the road, I managed to avoid them and walk all the way home past the Factory and Nantlle Vale Football Club. Such a day was a good day.

Before long, I started to mitch school in the mornings.

About eleven o' clock every day I'd be starving and I just had to go and look for something to eat. Normally a cake or a pie from the shop in the main street would ease the pain, but only temporarily. Before long the wrenching feeling in my stomach would return with a vengeance. The pain, most probably, was a sign of the psychological and emotional effect of the bullying, and I tried to ease it by eating more and more. I didn't know the word 'bulimia' at the time, but that's what it was. I'd already started to look for ways of escaping from these uncomfortable feelings – avoiding reality. I had also started to steal. The pocket money I was given wasn't much; as a family we were a little strapped for cash, as I mentioned before. But my mother's purse was always full of coins and if I couldn't steal from her, it was easy enough to grab a cake from the shop.

A few days before the end of my first term at the secondary school a certain affair caused a radical and permanent change in life at the manse. I brought home my first school report, which was a shocker! I was placed twenty-third in the class and, needless to say, this was a grave disappointment to my parents. We went through the marks for each subject, one by one, and each one resulting in cross words. For some reason, my father had expected me to come at least third – not twenty-third – and he couldn't hide the fact that he'd lost all faith in me, and all regard for me. That's when he started nagging me about having to become a quarryman. He put my failure down to not reading enough. And he may have been right, because I hated reading (though I remember reading *Lady Chatterley's Lover* with relish!), but he had no notion of my growing tendency to want to do the exact opposite of what he wanted me to do. It came to an end with a stern warning that I had to do better; Rowenna had gone to college, Arwel was doing well in the Sixth Form, and I was the only cause for concern – their only disappointment. That was drummed into me until it became an indelible mark on my mind.

By the summer exams the situation was no better; the marks were just as disastrous, which prompted more dishonesty on my part. If the marks were to remain as they were the prospect of enjoying the summer holidays was not good! So, I decided to doctor all the lowest marks. In Latin 28 became 58; in Chemistry 15 became 95; and 33 in French became 88. Unfortunately, I scratched the paper slightly as I changed one figure and this caused the ink to smudge. My heart was beating hard with trepidation when I arrived home to face the music. They were waiting for me, both of them, in the kitchen, ready to begin the inquisition.

The forgery wasn't spotted at first and for a few minutes I enjoyed the most unusual praise. Then, suddenly, my mother screamed:

"Rachmaninov! This report's been changed!"

"What did you say, woman?" said Dad as he snatched the report, the blood draining from his face.

"Look!" said Mam, "This mark's supposed to be twenty eight, not fifty eight!"

Before they could say any more I ran out of the room and rushed upstairs to the bathroom. In a hysterical state I opened the cupboard and saw a dark bottle with a label saying, 'Caution. Caustic substance. Avoid contact with eyes.' Without giving it a second thought I splashed some of the stuff into my eyes. The pain was excruciating and I screamed the place down. I then took the blade out of my father's razor, sat on the toilet and began slashing my wrists. Mam and Dad rushed in – and had the shock of their lives. They rushed me to Dr. Tom Ellis's surgery in Pen-y-groes and he was able to ease the pain and stop the bleeding. When things had calmed down, the doctor asked me, quietly: "Why did you do this, Wynford?"

"I don't know, Doctor," I replied. But that was a lie, too, because I knew very well what it was – it was 'diversionary tactics' – tactics I was to use many a time after that.

Although those actions were prompted by the row about the report, I had been feeling depressed for a long time. Only a few days before that incident, I'd written these words (in Welsh): 'Life has no purpose any more; it is uninteresting and unimportant. One may struggle to find some purpose in life, but me? I have tried ... and failed.'

The case of the forged report was allowed to rest – in full view on top of the dresser, just as a reminder! All things considered, I had a fairly good summer – staying with Mr. Jones the Carpenter in Liverpool. But things weren't quite right. I couldn't get my act of deceit out of my mind, and there were feelings of guilt and shame gnawing at my guts. The evil dragon was awake, smiling as its future plans for me were beginning to take shape. These destructive emotions were to leave me completely devastated later in life.

During my stay at Liverpool I had my first taste of alcohol. It was only a bottle of Babycham but it was enough to convince me that the resolution I'd made to taste alcohol as soon as I'd escaped the shackles of Llanllyfni, was worth keeping. I'd been shopping with Mrs. Jones and persuaded her to buy three bottles of the innocuous cider. (I realise, now, that there's no such thing as innocuous cider – well, not for me, anyway!) When we got home I made a grand ceremony of laying out the posh glasses, opening the tops and gently pouring, watching in amazement as the myriad of bubbles exploded; then there was the thrill of sniffing the sweet, mystical aroma of alcohol. And all this before I tasted a drop! There was, of course, the additional, devilish pleasure of doing something that was forbidden at home.

The extra-curricular aspect of school life wasn't too bad, especially during the *eisteddfodau*, when my performing talents were given the chance to flourish. I liked sport in general – I enjoyed cricket, was quite good at the high jump, long jump and the triple jump, and I was quite an accomplished goal-keeper. Indeed, I had a trial for the Wales under-15 team and was one of the top four keepers. I tried my hand at rugby, too, but the standard of rugby in North Wales wasn't very high at that time, and when the school team lost heavily against a team from South Wales in the Urdd competition, it knocked the stuffing out of me! But the performing arts were my forte, and I made the most of every opportunity.

For three glorious weeks in the Spring Term every year, school life revolved around the *eisteddfod*, with the four houses, Llifon, Llyfnwy, Silyn and Dulyn, competing for the coveted prize. I was in Llyfnwy, and whilst the other houses did well in other competitions such as sport, Llyfnwy always did particularly well in the *eisteddfod*. I was fully committed, taking part in everything from singing and reciting to whistling and yodelling! I even sang a duet with Meira, my future wife, although we weren't sweethearts at the time! Another person who was equally committed to winning the *eisteddfod* for Llyfnwy was Matt Pritchard, the History teacher. It's strange how individuals can be two different people in different environments. In class I just didn't get on with her; perhaps I lacked concentration but I couldn't make head or tail of all the information she plastered all over the blackboard and, as was common practice in those days, satire and ridicule formed a prominent part of her teaching style. When it came to the *eisteddfod*, though, both she and I were different persons and we got on like a house on fire. She was an inspiring leader, and because I was so enthusiastic she took a keen personal interest in me. I thrived in that situation, and the opportunity to act various parts – in other words, to be anything or anyone other than my true self – was too good to miss. Performing, for me, was easy; my problem was living a normal life.

It surprised no one, therefore, that I starred in school productions such as *Midsummer Night's Dream*, in English, in which I played Peter Quince, and J. T. Jones's wonderful translation of *The Merchant of Venice*, in which I played the part of Shylock. Public speaking was another field in which I excelled – in both Welsh and English. I once won the British public speaking competition, in Newtown, with my friend, Beti Williams, who later became MP for Conwy, as chairman. I have to acknowledge my father's contribution to my success in public speaking; he was my scriptwriter and he was marvellous at it.

It is in connection with public speaking that I have one of

the most horrible memories of the headmaster, Mr. R. H. Pritchard-Jones. I had just won the Urdd Public Speaking competition held at the Reardon Smith Lecture Theatre in Cardiff. The Dyffryn Nantlle School team was judged to be the best in the national final – Ann Lloyd Edwards as chairman, Alwyn Humphreys proposing the vote of thanks and me as the speaker. The subject was 'Ladies' Fashions', and Dad had written me a cracking speech, witty and humorous.

Soon afterwards a Grand Concert was held at the school and, as a tribute to the public speaking team's astonishing success, we were invited to repeat our performance as an item in the programme. On the stage that night, Mr. Pritchard-Jones shook my hand and said some very complimentary things about me to the audience; how proud he was of me, and how I was a credit to the school and the whole neighbourhood. And whilst the audience showed their appreciation he turned to me and said: "You realise, don't you, boy, that I didn't mean a word of what I said!"

That remark was deeply hurtful and it took years for me to get it out of my system. The most damaging thing about it was that it consolidated an impression that had been forming in my mind for some time – that I couldn't trust people in authority; that they were two-faced, saying one thing and meaning another. This feeling persisted into my adulthood; I felt uncomfortable in the presence of people in authority. I felt inferior, doubtful of their motives, and I was disrespectful of them.

But the above incident was only one of many. Throughout my time in the secondary school, the headmaster subjected me to almost daily bullying. He delighted in intimidating me in front of my class and the whole school. He was a small man, physically, (that's why the pupils called him 'Pritch Bach'), but very loud. You could hear his footsteps miles away, and he wore a black gown, which added to his fearsome presence. He was a brilliant teacher of his subject – I had some experience of that – and, I must say, outside the school situation he was quite gentlemanly towards me. He and my father were friends – they'd gone to the same college – and I was always afraid he'd tell my father how badly I was doing at school! (But then, Dad knew that anyway!) However, in school, I was afraid of him and I was convinced that Mr. R. H. Pritchard-Jones was no friend of mine.

I have a theory to explain this. Looking back at those days, I have come to the conclusion that the headmaster had recognised the alcoholic trait in me – although he didn't know what it was at the time. What I mean is that he'd sensed the 'defiance' in me, which is a characteristic of all alcoholics. He reacted to that defiance by being nasty to me and trying to undermine my apparent haughtiness in an effort to change me. That is the only explanation I can think of for his strange behaviour towards me. But even that appears rather magnanimous in the context of his parting words to me when I left school: "I won't wish you good luck, boy – you don't deserve it!" Perhaps he was, after all, just a bully.

This continual bullying was a very daunting experience. It was made a hundred times worse by the fact that I couldn't confide in anyone. No one would have listened to me; the pendulum was very much in the teachers' favour then, quite different from the situation today. It shouldn't surprise anyone, therefore, to know that during this difficult period in my life I tried to deal with my problem by running away – not literally, but by escaping into the distorted, perplexed and perverse world of my imagination – helped by my mother's strong sleeping pills.

Now and again my mother would discover that some of her tablets were missing, and there'd be a hell of a row, but I often got away with denying any involvement. (Later in life I used to do that when I'd been drinking, insisting to Meira and the children that I hadn't touched a drop, although I was quite drunk and incoherent – a perfect example of the condition known as 'denial'. Alcoholism is one of the few illnesses that tell the sufferer there is nothing wrong with him or her.) There were times when I was caught red-handed, and then I'd be taken to see the GP. He, in turn, would try to persuade me of the dangers of taking such strong drugs – although he admitted that 90% of the population of Dyffryn Nantlle were on sedatives at the time. But no one ever tried to dissuade Mam from taking them – and what was good enough for Mam was good enough for me!

Anyway, by then, I'd become psychologically addicted to these tablets. I was no longer dependent on the whims of others for approval or love etc. to make me feel good about myself. The tablets enabled me to change my mood completely. I took two tablets before going to bed and then suddenly, all the tension in my body would disappear; my pains and troubles would simply evaporate. Living was a pleasure once again, and I'd found an effective short cut to feeling good. The opportunity to flee to this happy land every night was too good to miss, even to please Mam and Dad, let alone any GP. The thick head the following day was no deterrent, either. It was worth it – to escape each night from the real world, and from the dragon that was by now fully awake all day every day, eagerly waiting to be fed with the barbiturates. Unfortunately, Mam had become wary of the disappearing pills and had started to count them regularly, making my task of stealing them almost impossible. That was when I became a friend of the elderly in the village.

One old lady whom I befriended had recently been widowed and was afraid of staying in the house on her own. I slept at her house for several months to keep her company, but I had an ulterior motive. The doctor had prescribed strong sleeping tablets to help her cope with her grief and, of course, I was able to help myself! She never suspected a thing. And there were others, too, who unwittingly provided me with a plentiful supply of drugs. During this period, I swallowed all kinds of pills – for high blood pressure, low blood pressure, water retention, kidney, bladder, bowel problems etc. – and suffered all kinds of side effects! Despite the ulterior motive, my relationship with these elderly people, all of them living on their own, developed into true and lasting friendship.

In those heady days of the early 1960s, when John F. Kennedy was assassinated in Dallas, Texas; man's first landing on the moon; the Beatles sweeping to world-wide popularity, and the Rolling Stones frightening every parent in the land with their shocking behaviour and hedonistic attitudes, there was one young man who was already a slave to drugs – and he lived, not in trendy Carnaby Street, but at The Manse, Rhedyw Road, Llanllyfni!

My father was an old-fashioned Nonconformist minister,

set in traditional Christian values and true to the old, narrow-minded, Welsh way of life. But the world about us was changing fast, becoming more secular and materialistic. John Lennon's notorious claim that 'The Beatles are more popular than Jesus Christ!' caused a stir, but it was a sign of the times. And there, in the middle, was I – torn between my father's yesterday and tomorrow's new world – not knowing which road to take. I tried to live in both worlds, and that was one of the greatest mistakes of my life, because the only way I could manage that was by being a hypocrite – and hypocrisy, like living a lie, is the most emotionally painful way to exist. The emotional pain that resulted from my trying to be something I was not, was sometimes almost unbearable.

It was about this time that I went on a weekend religious course at Glyn Llifon College – one of three pupils selected to represent the school. All in all it was a good weekend and, yes, the boys were caught in the girls' room in the middle of the night! It was quite an innocuous event, really – crisps and Dandelion & Burdock, and creepy stories and jokes – but rules had been broken and that warranted being marched downstairs to stand in a row in our pyjamas to be reprimanded. Fair enough. And, as befitted a religious course, we learned something about God, as well – the God of retribution and revenge, as was the popular concept of the time.

Back in school on the Monday morning, however, the harmless escapade of the weekend was to be interpreted as a heinous attempt to undermine the whole of the education system and a betrayal of all the principles the school stood for. And, most serious of all, we had offended Pritch Bach, the Head! The three of us were hauled before a disciplinary panel and made to feel that we were the greatest sinners on earth. It was a grossly humiliating experience, out of all proportion to the offence, and the feeling of injustice was acute. Things weren't too good between me and Pritch Bach before, but from that day on we might as well have lived on two different planets. Not a word was spoken between us until the day I left school, when he shook my hand and uttered those cruel words that I didn't deserve to be wished good luck. The three 'culprits' had to write a letter to the Head to apologise for the misdemeanours of the weekend, and then we had to take the letter home to be signed by our parents. My letter was signed by Miss World, bless her, and my parents never heard a thing about it!

When the time came to move on to the Sixth Form I was found wanting, just a little bit! I'd passed five subjects at O Level, but that wasn't enough to proceed to study three A Level subjects, as was the norm. However, I was allowed to enter Form Six for one year – to catch up on some O Levels and to follow the A Level course in Welsh and English, without any intention, obviously, of sitting the exams. I may appear to be paranoid about this, but I do feel strongly about people being labelled as failures early on, and the resulting lack of expectation being a major contributing factor in eventual underachievement by those people. That certainly happened in my case. The teachers in the secondary school, right from the start, branded me as dull, and made no attempt to investigate any possible reasons for my apparent backwardness. My parents, too, had lost every faith and aspiration for me after the affair of the falsified report. I felt at the time, and I still feel it, that I was let down by the education system; it was so set and blinkered, unable to acknowledge or encourage or develop any interest or talent outside the confines of the old, traditional fields of study.

In those days the O Level results were published in the local newspapers. So you can imagine the shame that descended like a black cloud over the manse on the morning it was announced to the world that the local minister's son had 'failed'. What to do next was the burning question. My father suggested that I should go and work in the quarry, but my mother's response to that was: "Ye gods, Bob! Leave off! Hyacinth can't do that!"

It was Rowenna, who was about to be married and move to live in Bolton, who came up with the most sensible answer. "You like acting and performing on the stage, Wyn," she said, "Why don't you go to a drama college or something like that?" It made sense! The only time I'd ever been able to please my parents was when I was acting in the Action Song or performing in the public speaking competitions. I had always wanted so much to please them ... but ... perhaps this was it! In addition to pleasing my parents it would also help me to overcome my increasing self-deprecation – I'd become embarrassingly conscious of my big nose, and felt extremely awkward in female company. Acting, being someone else, seemed a very good idea.

The well-known playwright, Huw Lloyd Edwards, taught me two great Shakespearian speeches and off I went to London to seek fame and fortune! But I was quickly brought down to earth! First of all, I discovered there was quite a gap between my strong Welsh accent and 'Standard English', which seemed to be the only form acceptable at the time. But my youth was also against me. "Sorry. Not this time. Try in a few years' time, when you're older!"

'A few years' time?' I'd be mad by then if I didn't escape from Llanllyfni!

The Welsh College of Music and Drama in Cardiff was brought to my attention. They offered a combined acting and teacher-training course. The teacher-training element appealed to my father. "It's important for you to have something to fall back on, Jac-y-do – and you can get a grant for that, as well!" I was interviewed by Raymond Edwards, the Principal, and we immediately clicked. He was a good sort. At the same time, I was accepted at Cyncoed College (UWIC, today) to follow up my drama course with teacher training – although I had no intention of becoming a teacher.

With that settled, then, all I had to do was to wait patiently until I was eighteen – a rather difficult task for someone who was hyperactive! The Beatles were topping the charts everywhere, and if they could do it, what was to stop an equally talented group of lads from Dyffryn Nantlle? Enter Pavlov's Hounds!

Pavlov had four Hounds – Ian Damerell, John Leighton, Twm Elias and me. We formed a decent rock 'n roll group, and we certainly looked the part with our long hair (well, everyone except me – I wasn't allowed to grow my hair long). I was the singer and, although I say it myself, I was pretty good! Chuck Berry was one of our favourites but our real idols were the Rolling Stones – they were so unconventional and anti-establishment. We practised regularly, every week, and now and again on a Friday night we held dances at the Drill Hall in Caernarfon, which were very popular.

My brother, Arwel, was by now a student at the University of Wales, Aberystwyth, and was the social secretary of the Students' Union. (A year later he was to become President.) He was obviously aware of Pavlov's Hounds and he invited us to take part in one of the college hops at the famous King's Hall – for a fee of seventeen pounds! We practised hard, not only to deserve the fee, but also in order to impress. Who knew where this 'break' might lead?

Anyway, we arrived at Aberystwyth quite early and the boys wanted to go for a pint! I tried to stop them – because I knew instinctively that drinking alcohol and performing don't mix – but I was outnumbered, and off we went. I didn't drink any alcohol myself for I was still faithful to my resolution not to until I'd left home. Also, I was afraid of being seen drinking by Arwel, and really scared that Mam and Dad would find out. I'm not sure what I was afraid would happen, because my parents never gave me a hiding, or even threatened me, physically. And yet they were able to exercise this hold on me – that I should never drink, or be seen drinking.

Unbeknown to me, when I started taking Mam's sleeping tablets, I turned my back on the God that had been drilled into me as a child. I became dependent on my own devices to find the feel-good factor. I was drifting through life like a rudder-less ship at the mercy of the elements; I had no control, and that is what gave rise to all my fears. But I wouldn't have to wait long, now, before finding an alternative god – another, seemingly more efficient god that would take away all my fears – alcohol!

Meantime, back at the King's Hall, Pavlov's Hounds were first on stage – and things weren't going exactly to plan.

People weren't taking to the floor and we thought perhaps it was too early in the evening but, alas, it seemed that we were not up to expectation. Complaints had been made to the organising committee, of which Arwel was the chairman, and he had the unpleasant task of informing me that we had to leave. Our fee would be paid in full, but we had to leave, there and then! The Pavlov's Hounds dream was well and truly smashed!

On the Wednesday night a few days before I left home to become a student at the College of Music and Drama, Dad was watching his favourite programme on TV – wrestling, with Ken Walton as commentator. As usual, he was full of action, still sitting in his armchair, but punching and kicking the air with Mick McManus and the others.

Suddenly, he stood up and switched the sound off. He then turned to me and said, in a quiet and serious tone: "Wynford, if I ever hear that you've been drinking, I'll break my heart." With that, he switched the sound on again and went back to his wrestling.

I was completely flattened. What about my vow, once free from this puritanical environment, to partake of the forbidden cup? Now, with that solitary statement, my father had ruined everything, because the last thing I wanted was to break his heart.

My father was a good man and you couldn't help but respect him. He was tall and always smartly dressed; his soft voice, his demeanour, his wisdom, his honesty, his utter dedication to his ministry – everything about him demanded respect. He had a sense of humour, too, and he'd often use that humour to good effect in his hard-hitting sermons from the pulpit. Tommy Cooper and Sergeant Bilko were his favourites – and mine, as it happens! And yet, he was a quiet man, very serious, and deeply affected by his deafness. Because he wasn't afraid to speak his mind, even if it offended people, some thought he was a hard and insensitive man. I thought so for a period. It was much later that I realised that my father – and Mam, too – in their own ways, only wanted the best for me.

But one thing was very clear in my mind in September 1966 as I prepared to leave Llanllyfni and its unhappy memories and head for Cardiff – I had no intention whatsoever of hurting my father's feelings. I pushed the vow to the back of my mind and, strangely, I felt no urge to drink alcohol. None whatsoever, and I made him a promise to that effect with my hand firmly on the Bible.

1966 1969

HEADY COLLEGE DAYS

'Son of a North Wales manse on drugs charges in Cardiff.' The shame! What would Mam and Dad say?

My father had written to the Rev. Dr. Lodwig Jones, B.A., B.D., the Minister at Crwys Chapel, Cardiff, to let him know that I was on the way – and many more of Cardiff's leading religious figures had received a similar notice. These contacts would prove to be very useful at a later date.

The Welsh College of Music and Drama was located within the walls of Cardiff Castle. Very impressive! On the very first day of the new term I arrived early, full of excitement. I was aware, of course, that I was following in the footsteps of no less an actor than Anthony Hopkins! I remember being disappointed that hardly any of the students were Welsh-speaking; there were only about four throughout the college. Welsh within the college has gained a much higher status since then – in response to the increased demand and opportunities for Welsh-language actors – but at the time, the main product was fodder for the English theatre and television.

Anyway, the thirty or so students in my group were a great bunch. But while they spent the evenings socialising at the Horse & Groom, the 'official' college pub in Womanby Street across the road, I spent my time on my own in my bed-sit in Allensbank Road in Heath. This went on for three long weeks, and I hated the banter in the common room every morning, with comments like: "Where were you last night, Wyn? You missed a bloody good night!" Once again I started to see myself as the outsider looking in – never a part of anything; not belonging. I was full of self-pity, but my father's words kept ringing in my ears: "Wyn, I'll break my heart if I hear you've been drinking!" I just couldn't do that to him. Despite the growing temptation, I was able to resist – just because of those words. But, on the fourth Monday of the term, after three whole weeks of agony, I relented and joined the crew in the Horse & Groom. Needless to say, I got drunk. At last I had found my real 'home'.

That first night was a spiritual experience for me. (They don't call alcohol 'spirits' for nothing!) Suddenly, I found that I didn't despise myself any more; I was full of love towards my fellow men, and they loved me, too. My long, crooked nose didn't bother me any more – alcohol had made it straight and transformed me into Adonis. I became the life and soul of the party! I was comfortable with myself and, suddenly, I even enjoyed the company of young ladies. There was no embarrassment or self-consciousness whatsoever. Tomorrow was full of hope – and I was free! Released from my past; relieved of all my frustrations and fears; brimming with confidence and, most important of all, I experienced the feeling of belonging – that sense of one-ness. No longer was I on the outside looking in, but inside, in the centre, where I really belonged. At last I felt that I mattered – I was at one with the world and at one with my new god!

It was, indeed, a truly spiritual experience! Some people call alcoholism 'the sacred illness' for that reason – it mimics the real spiritual experience to a tee. The only difference is how long it lasts. In my case, by the morning after, the 'heavenly' feeling had gone, allowing all the old fears and negative feelings to flood back into my mind – with the added feeling of guilt and shame at having broken my promise to my father.

So, there was only one thing for it – a repeat performance on the Tuesday night! And so began the mad merry-go-round.

After that I never went to The Horse & Groom, or any pub or club, without the sole intention of getting drunk. Not to have a few pints, but to change the mood – to drink myself stupid and escape from the real world. The effect of too much alcohol on 'normal' people, after the initial high, is to make them sleepy or sick, but with the alcoholic it's quite different. The body feels a physical allurement* to the alcohol; it makes the adrenalin flow; it brings us to life – we are fired up, and it changes our perspective of reality.

But why do alcoholics want to escape from the real world? Why do they want to flee from themselves?

The simple answer is to do with the issue of low self-esteem. Addicts feel disgusted with their behaviour whilst under the influence, and they want to block out the memory. The only cure for the active addict is another drink or drug, thus leading to more bad behaviour resulting in the further lowering of their self-worth.

Coupled with this is the awful sense of aloneness that alcoholics feel. The more they deny their true feelings to themselves, the more divorced they become from their authentic selves. This pain of separateness, or duality, between their physical and spiritual self (their sense of values, morals and conscience) is at the core of addiction. It's this pain of duality that they try to kill stone dead with alcohol and/or other mood-altering substances and behaviour.

But there may be a more deep-rooted psychological explanation. I believe that a person's emotional development is stymied as soon as he or she begins using mood-altering substances and behaviour, be it alcohol, drugs, sex, misuse of

---

*In Alcoholics Anonymous literature dealing with this particular matter, the term used to describe this reaction is allergy.

food (all four in my case), or gambling, work, controlling other people etc. etc. (There's a long list of things that affect a person's mood.) The result is that the addict can be a very immature person. In my case, when I started taking my mother's sleeping pills I had found a short cut to feeling good. I didn't have to go through the normal cognitive process of 'thinking' myself into a good mood. So, at the age of twelve, I stopped developing emotionally. And when I was an eighteen-year-old man I had the emotions of a twelve-year-old – easily hurt and offended, sulking, defiant, hating, jealous, quarrelsome... These emotions can be extremely painful, and it is little wonder that the addict will seek a means of escape.

Alcoholics will often swear never to drink again, claiming that the withdrawal pain following the last drunken session was too much to bear ever again. But the mind feeds a different message to the brain, deleting all memory of the pain and forming a delusion that things will be better next time; better performance – in work and in bed – better sleep, better ... everything! And as soon as they have the next drink, the physical attraction to alcohol kicks in, along with the mental preoccupation ('how', 'where' and 'when'), and the process begins all over again. The only way to stop that insane merry-go-round is to stop taking alcohol – to refuse that first drink. It's that first drink or drug that does the damage. Once that happens it is almost impossible to control the urge.

However, strange as it may seem, stopping drinking is the least of the alcoholic's problems. Had my problem been simply alcohol I could have found an easy cure – stop drinking! But the problem wasn't alcohol – it was alcoholism.

I don't drink alcohol these days, but I believe I'm still an alcoholic. The illness, and the emotional suffering that goes with it, is still with me. What I've done by not taking alcohol is to remove one of the symptoms of alcoholism – but in doing so, I have broken the circuit and the merry-go-round has stopped.

It could be started up again, though, quite easily. I'm not cured. I accept there is no cure for alcoholism. 'Once an alcoholic, always an alcoholic.' I understand, also, that it is a progressive and fatal illness; it gets worse with time, never better. What this means is that if an alcoholic gives up alcohol for a period of time, even a few years, once he or she takes that first drink, they will find themselves, within a relatively short time, drinking as much as they did when they first came into recovery.

So, in addition to making sure I don't take that first drink – or, rather, in order to make sure I don't take that first drink – I have to control the emotional aspect of the illness and become reconciled with my past. This involves looking at my way of thinking and behaving – learning to deal appropriately with my anger, to overcome my fears and resentments, learning to be assertive and become a risk taker by being willing to show people who I really am. It also means making amends for wrongs done in the past. In other words, I have to 'toughen up'.

It's been a challenge. It still is, and frankly, it's a challenge I couldn't cope with on my own. How can any alcoholic cope with such a challenge without the help of some 'power' or other? Before giving it up, alcohol was the power in their lives; that's what subdued all the crude emotions.

Having lost all faith and trust in themselves and others, they put their faith absolutely in the power of the bottle. What now, then, without the bottle?

I had been brought up, obviously, in the Christian faith, and as a child I had accepted God without any question. The doubts began when that God didn't answer my prayers – I prayed for Him to stop my mother from taking those sleeping pills and the awful senna pods which made her so ill, and I prayed for Him to stop Pritch Bach, my headmaster, from bullying me. And anyway, He was the God of vengeance and punishment, the God of my father's puritanical, cruel, Welsh way of life, which I hated so much. Then, when I discovered the 'power' of my mother's sleeping pills to give me comfort and solace, I inadvertently turned my back on God. I had found an alternative god – a god that seemed much more willing and much better equipped to cater for my needs.

Little did I know then that one day I would need to find another power, a power greater than myself or any human being, a power stronger than alcohol, even, if I was to have any hope of conquering alcoholism. That's the deal for all of us who really want to recover – we cannot rely on our own resources. We've tried that, endlessly, and it never works. We have to discover some other power to restore our spiritual values: faith, hope, honesty and trust – the values we lost because of our addiction.

There are as many different ideas about the higher power as there are addicts in recovery. I chose God as my higher power because it fitted in with my upbringing, and was familiar to me.

It's a fair assumption to think that most alcoholics will

have turned their backs on God – or their own version of a god – at some stage on the way to becoming a full-blown alcoholic. But it is also a fair assumption that most alcoholics find it impossible to stop drinking by depending on our own will power. We need the help of some other 'power' if we are to recover. This 'power' need not have anything to do with religion – it is just a power that exists outside our own mind, and greater than our own mind, but it's a power we need to cooperate with in order to help us in the process of recovery. And the good thing is that it is there, within the grasp of each and every one of us who really wants to recover – if we are willing to accept it. And that is the key to the whole process – 'acceptance'. Unfortunately, acceptance does not come easily. The alcoholic can be a very stubborn person!

'Denial' is another symptom of the illness of alcoholism – the state of mind in which you will deny there is anything wrong with you, despite all the evidence to the contrary! Denial is actually a psychological 'coping strategy'. It is something not only addicts engage in. People who are not addicts, also, suffer from denial about all sorts of things. The reason it is so particularly devastating with regards to addiction is that it is much harder to break down because of the huge investment in what it is protecting – or the high stakes if you like – to the addict. Active addicts genuinely believe that they cannot live a comfortable, pain-free life without their drug of choice.

It's a difficult situation. In spite of the 'denial' syndrome, the realisation and the acceptance of the need for help must come from inside. It may take a long time, and it may involve a lot of suffering, but come it will, in the end – when the body and the mind and the spirit cannot take any more punishment. At that moment, and not until then – for those who survive that long – the soul will scream out the most earnest of prayers, 'H-e-l-p!'.

The first step is for the alcoholic to accept, totally and genuinely, that he or she is an alcoholic and that they need help. Then they must accept a number of other things. They must accept themselves as a person, as they really are – feelings, needs, desires, the state they are in, including all their problems, where they live, where they work and the quality of their work. This need not be all doom and gloom. In every situation, no matter how bleak or hopeless, there is always something positive lurking underneath the surface, if you look for it! The next step, then, is to accept other people – again, as they are – and consider the quality of the relationship with these people.

Acceptance, therefore, is the catalyst that makes change possible. It brings peace of mind and satisfaction; it opens the door to a better world and allows the alcoholic to move on. It enables them to consider what needs to be done in order to take control of the situation – to take care of themselves, and to begin confronting 'the burden of being human'.

Blackouts are another feature of alcoholism, where the sufferer is unable to recollect or explain what happened during the period of drunkenness. All alcoholics suffer blackouts from time to time. They can go about their daily work, enter into a relationship with another person or even go on holiday to the Costa del Sol – and be totally oblivious to it all! I could remember nothing about that great first night in the Horse & Groom – it's other people who told me I'd had a great night! But in those early days, in 1966, the fact that I couldn't remember what had happened the night before didn't concern me at all. That was to come later, about two years down the line, when I worked for the BBC. I was there for eighteen months, apparently, but I can recollect hardly anything that happened to me in the damn place!

Anyway, after the 'induction', the Horse & Groom became like a magnet – I was drawn back there every day, even at lunchtime. After a liquid lunch of several pints I'd be sick against the pub wall in Womanby Street before staggering across the road to the college to fall asleep or be a nuisance at the back of the lecture room. I threw myself into the college social life with great zest, more drinking in the Horse & Groom in the evenings or partying in various flats until the small hours of the morning.

When I wasn't drinking, I began to feel a strange tension inside me, as if there was a spring in my stomach being stretched and stretched. The pain would become almost unbearable, like toothache. I'd be obsessed with it, and become completely self-centred. When the terrible tragedy happened at Aberfan,* I felt my pain was as great as that of those poor people, if not greater! And the only solution was to drink – because alcohol was the only thing that could ease that horrible spring inside me and relieve the tension.

All this drinking had little effect on my general health. My stomach suffered when I drank too much but not enough to make me stop – oh no! In a strange way, the more I drank, the less aware I became of the pain. I also noticed that if I

---

*The Aberfan disaster occurred on October 21st 1966. Coal waste rushed down the mountainside destroying houses and a school. 144 people were killed, including half the children in the school and five of their teachers.

drank spirits (whisky and rum & black were the favourites), instead of beer and larger, my stomach didn't protest so much. So, I took to drinking shorts – killing two birds with one stone: getting drunk quicker and getting medication for my stomach!

And how, you might ask, was I able to afford all this wild drinking? Well, I was on full grant, since my father's salary was so meagre. But that wasn't enough, by far, and I had to find another source of income. Alcoholics are good at this kind of thing. They are usually very resourceful people, clever, intelligent, with the ability and potential to earn big money. That is important to them, not only for the prestige which feeds their pride (only an alcoholic can look down upon the world from the gutter!), but also in order to fund the drinking, which can be very expensive. And so I became a regular worshiper at Crwys Road, Cardiff's very grand Calvinistic Methodist chapel. The intention was not so much to meet God but rather some other people, more important than God, who frequented the place at the time. That is where some of the BBC bigwigs went to worship!

One Sunday morning I had a word with one of them – Owen Edwards, who was presenter of the popular TV news magazine programme, *Heddiw* (Today). I asked him where I should go to look for work, and where was this Broadway I'd heard so much about. At the time, I must admit, I thought that Sammy Davis Junior and Frank Sinatra performed there – but that was a different Broadway! This one was an old chapel in Broadway, off Newport Road, where the BBC studios in Cardiff were housed. Another chapel! You couldn't get away from God's chapels in those days!

Anyway, Crwys Road, with all its media connections, was obviously the place to be! So, I became a faithful 'Christian'. That was no problem at all. I was a dab hand at playing the hypocrite. I even preached there one Sunday evening – I'd borrowed one of my father's sermons and delivered it with conviction. I almost sparked off a revival, I'm sure!

I moved from my flat in Allensbank Road to live with my brother, Arwel, and Hywel Gwynfryn, the well-known Welsh-language broadcaster, in Ninian Park Road. This was a bittersweet experience. Arwel's move to Cardiff caused me some uneasiness. He'd been offered a post, straight from college, with the BBC programme, *Heddiw* – and he was trespassing on my patch. Performing, appearing on television, was *my* field, and I was jealous of his early success. I was also afraid of him, and his presence reminded me of my immediate past and the narrow upbringing that I'd only recently escaped from. It was like living with George Orwell's 'big brother' who literally kept me under his supervision. Fortunately, he was away quite a lot with his work and didn't stay in the flat much. But I still felt that he was an extension of my parents' influence and that he was there for the sole purpose of keeping an eye on me! I felt I had to try and control my drinking. I dare not give Arwel, or Hywel, or anybody else, any indication of how hooked I really was on alcohol.

Hywel was great fun. Every week he'd have a different bee in his bonnet, a fad in which he'd immerse himself completely. One week it would be a drum set, and he'd thump these drums till late in the night, keeping us all awake; the following week it would be photography, and he was determined to be better at it than Anthony Armstrong-Jones; then it would be keeping fit, and so on and so on. He seemed to be a person who was searching for something in life, as I was. But unlike me, he enjoyed what he was doing and perhaps that was his anchor – he had found his vocation. Would I have turned out differently if I'd had the same kind of focus? I doubt it, somehow, because my illness was genetic.

There are many alcoholics who are able to lead a normal life for a long time – treading on thin ice, as it were. They drink excessively, but their minds are still able to function fairly sensibly – until one day they cross that invisible line which differentiates between drinking because you *want* to, and drinking because you *have* to. Then the most potent drug of all takes over. They then sink to the depths of alcoholism and suffer the horrible and all-too-familiar consequences – they lose their health, their self-respect, homes, families, their sanity and even their lives, if they are lucky.

My type of alcoholism is different. Alcoholism, I believe, is in my genes. I was born an alcoholic, with a predisposition to misuse alcohol. Therefore from the moment I first tasted alcohol, I drank like an alcoholic, out of control each time. But long before I even tasted alcohol, I had an alcoholic mind – warped – and functioning abnormally as if under the influence of drink. Ever since I was a child, therefore, my mind has been feeding me lies – giving me false information about life; making me imagine things; concealing the true facts. And on the basis of those false impressions I had given vent to my very immature emotions and behaved childishly. My behaviour was based on a false interpretation of things around me – believing my own lies; I had lost touch with the reality of life. Or to be exact, I had never been in touch with reality; the world I'd known had always been my imaginary world, a world of fantasy.

However, the lack of money to fund my drinking seemed real enough in my first year at the Welsh College of Music and Drama! Salvation came in the form of the BBC inter-college public speaking competition. This was a prestigious competition, and very popular at the time, with representatives from all the colleges in Wales competing for the accolade of best public speaker. I had excelled in this field before, of course, and that experience must have helped because I won the competition hands down, apparently! This result was important to me in many ways. It brought me popularity, which I craved, and the approval of the College Principal, Raymond Edwards; it propelled me into the world of broadcasting – and it also solved my short-term cash flow problem!

Soon afterwards, I was offered work as one of the many presenters on the HTV weekly current affairs programme, *Nos Wener* (Friday Night), hosted by the enigmatic Gwyn Erfyl. (He was an enigma to me because not only was he a well respected TV broadcaster and an acknowledged scholar, but also a minister of religion – and he drank alcohol in public! At the time he made me think that perhaps alcohol was not the demon my parents had made it out to be. I wished I'd met him many years earlier.) The work itself was easy enough. All I had to do was turn up at the studio in the afternoon, go over the links that had been prepared for me, and then read them on auto-cue as the programme was broadcast live later in the evening. It was OK and I enjoyed the work, especially the extra money to fund my drinking and hedonistic life-style. But one night the auto-cue broke down when I was in the middle of reading a news item about Harold Wilson – as I well remember.

I lost my grasp on what I was reading; I didn't know where I was. The old fears about my dyslexia came flooding back; the words in the text on my desk jumped about and I panicked. I didn't know what I was saying. I was saved further embarrassment when the item came up on the screen but the experience had shaken me to the core; my confidence had been shattered because I realised that I had a weakness which could strike at any time.

My way of coping with this problem, to try and make sure it didn't happen again, was to prepare thoroughly for every event. I became a perfectionist, and if you are a perfectionist yourself, or know someone who is, then you know what a dreadful thing it can be! The poor creature is under constant pressure, mostly self-imposed, and is never satisfied with anything. In the end perfectionists come to believe that they are indispensable, that nothing in the world can be right without their contribution – just like some of the people buried under grand tombstones in the local cemetery!

It's strange how some people react to other people's success. A few months after appearing on *Nos Wener* it was brought to the attention of the Caernarvonshire Education Authority, anonymously of course, that I was earning a salary whilst in receipt of a grant from the Authority. I had to repay some of the grant – which, unfortunately, I'd already spent. I was plunged even deeper in debt!

Although I was drunk most of the time, life at the college

was fairly uneventful. The only times I got into any trouble was when we argued about the Welsh language and its status within the college and in the education system generally at the time. It was at home, during college vacation, that life became difficult. I was like a lion in a cage; I was being stifled by the close community atmosphere of Llanllyfni. I felt I was being constantly watched, with people looking for any small sign of behaviour unbecoming of the son of the manse. How I longed to be back in the city and the freedom to be inconspicuous!

One night during the Christmas holiday I went to Caernarfon for a drink in the Royal Hotel. I felt so guilty, I went in through the back entrance in case someone saw me and told my parents! I was still afraid of my mum and dad, although I was allowed to smoke in their company by then. I downed two large vodkas. The effect was immediate: all the negative feelings and the painful tension and fears suddenly disappeared. And equally suddenly the reality of the situation dawned on me. For the first time in my life I realised that I was actually an alcoholic! It had crossed my mind before. I knew I was drinking too much – and that I couldn't help it. I'd realised for some time that I was getting too fond of the bottle, but on this particular night it struck me between the eyes that what I was doing just wasn't right – and I had to accept the fact that I was an alcoholic. I drove home slowly, deeply disturbed. What did this mean for me? What could I do about it?

I made a very important decision. As I was dropping off into a deep slumber with the aid of three of my mother's sleeping tablets, I promised myself that as soon as I got back to Cardiff, I'd find a GP to prescribe me some sleeping tablets like my mother's – so that I would have my own stock. I was convinced it would help me cut down on the drinking. After all, wasn't my failure to sleep one of my main reasons for getting drunk?

By the morning, however, I'd pushed the realisation about my alcoholism to the back of my mind. I buried it in that deep pit where I kept everything that was unacceptable or unpleasant to me. And that's where it remained until 1992. But I didn't ignore my promise to find a GP!

I registered with a local GP and persuaded him that my nerves were bad. Well, they were! I'd noticed that my hands were shaking in the morning – and that's another reason why I drank, to settle the nerves! Unfortunately, he wouldn't prescribe me strong sleeping tablets like Mam's – but he gave me Valium, which had a much worse long-term effect. From that moment onwards I swallowed sedatives and drank alcohol – and this went on for twenty-three years, during which time I also added sleeping tablets and antidepressants to the list. In the end I had three GPs giving me prescriptions, none aware of the others!

During one wild night at The Top Rank in Cardiff, with Dave Edmund's group, Love Sculpture, performing, I went to one of the side-rooms to swallow a handful of Valium tablets. I used to swallow them like Smarties – moderation wasn't part of my vocabulary! Suddenly a group of burly men appeared from nowhere, took the bottle from me and pushed me against the wall as if I was a member of the IRA. It turned out that they were members of the drug squad. The first thing that went through my mind was the news headlines – 'Son of a North Wales manse on drugs charges in Cardiff'. The shame! What would Mam and Dad say?

I had to give the performance of my life to avoid being arrested that night. "I'm sorry, officers, but I had one of my funny turns. Look, I'd have fainted from a panic attack if I hadn't taken my tablets. They are prescribed by my GP. Perhaps I should have stayed at home. That's what I normally do." It worked! My doctor gave me a telling off and a lecture on the dangers of behaving so irresponsibly, but there were no further repercussions – and my parents never found out.

Incidentally, the drug squad was set up in Britain initially to deal with the drug peddling of one particular young addict, hooked on heroin and alcohol, who provided drugs for all the Oxford colleges and the West End of London in the late 1950s – a man called Joe South. He then came to Wales to avoid police arrest and revenge attacks. He eventually sobered up and founded the treatment centre for addictive illnesses at Rhoserchan, near Aberystwyth. In fact, he is the one person mainly responsible for saving my life.

In my second year at the Welsh College of Music and Drama, the demands of the academic work began to interfere with my drinking. I had already appeared in several productions: *The Good Woman of Setzuan* and *Peer Gynt*, to name but two, and that was OK. And, fair play, I'd only missed about two performances because of the drink. During one production I drank so much that I lost my voice, and Peter Palmer, the producer, had to step in to take my place. But I blamed a bout of flu, and everyone believed me. I could still get away with monstrous lies in those early days.

I was fortunate enough to be given the part of the young lad in the BBC production of Gwenlyn Parry's play, *Tŷ ar y*

Tywod (A House Built on Sand). The cast included Stewart Jones, Brynley Jenkins, Guto Roberts and Lisabeth Miles – all top professional actors. But all I can remember of George P. Owen's production is that after the first recording session in the studio, I was called back from the BBC Club in Newport Road to do a re-take of one short scene. Of course, in the meantime, I'd been drinking, and I remember the look of disgust on everyone's faces when they realised I'd been drinking 'on duty'.

In college, I was told I had to write an extended essay before I could complete my course. Where the hell was I going to get the time to do something like that? My digs mate, John Greatorex, came up with a brilliant idea!

"Why don't you use my essay, Wynff?" he said. "You can doctor it here and there. No one will notice!"

"What's it about?" I asked.

"Eighteenth Century Melodrama. I wrote it for my finals in Bangor Normal. You can have it for ... two bottles of wine!"

It transpired that the same examiners who had given John a B- for his original efforts, gave me an A+! With that qualification safely under my belt, alcoholic poisoning in my blood, and with a growing feeling of guilt, off I went to Cyncoed College to become a qualified teacher!

In fact, I had the potential to be a very good teacher. With my enthusiasm and innate ability to inspire the kids' interest, I could get them to eat out of my hand. The only problem was, I couldn't keep it up for more than a few weeks. Perseverance has never been one of my strong points! I could never be a teacher – I wouldn't be able to sustain the effort. I couldn't see myself turning up at school day in day out. And there was another, more sinister reason – being in the company of pupils and other members of staff for any length of time would allow them to get to know me too well. I didn't want to allow anybody to get that close to me. I hid my true identity from everybody – even from myself, subconsciously!

Anyway, I had a prejudice against becoming a teacher. In my own little mind I had vowed that if ever I became a teacher, it would be because I'd failed as an actor. Teaching equated to failure on my part, and I never intended to be a teacher. The only reason I enrolled on the course was to satisfy the requirements of the grants system. Grants were available for attending universities or training colleges only. Drama college didn't qualify. But by following a course to become a drama teacher, I had the best of both worlds: two years in the drama college followed by one year in the training college. Right from the beginning, therefore, I had no intention of entering the teaching profession. I just 'used' the system and successfully hoodwinked the Education Authority.

I also hoodwinked the examiners into giving me a distinction in my teaching practice! As I said before, I could be inspirational in front of a class of pupils – for a brief period.

On the theory side of things, though, the situation was pretty grim. I only just managed to give in my written work in time. Six essays had been set at the beginning of the year but twenty-four hours from the deadline, I hadn't written a single syllable! I started writing at eight o' clock in the morning on the last day and worked all day and all night until seven o' clock the following morning – finishing one hour before the deadline! Such behaviour was characteristic of my total lack of self-discipline, which added immensely to the stress I already suffered.

Stress, I have found, is essential for the addict. They often go out of their way to create tension. That, in turn, justifies taking the first drink – because alcohol (or food, drugs, sex, whatever the addiction) is the only means of releasing that tension. Ironically, the 'drug' that addicts use to release the tension in them is, more often than not, the same as the one that causes the tension in the first place! The mad merry-go-round.

I realised that my whole lifestyle was chaotic, and I did try to get more organised. But the more I tried, the worse the result, and the stress increased. They say that an alcoholic's life is unmanageable. Things just go wrong – and that's how my life was. For example, I almost died at one stage during this period. I left the gas fire on all night, without any ventilation in the room, and was overcome by carbon monoxide. I was critically ill. I came to the conclusion that I needed someone to look after me!

With all alcoholics you will find – somewhere in the background – a wife or a husband, a partner, mother, someone very close, or sometimes even the family doctor! They are known as 'enablers'. Without the enablers' help, the alcoholic would find it impossible to carry on drinking and continue to have any semblance of a 'normal' life. The enablers look after the alcoholics, they nurse them, and they tidy up the mess – both literally and emotionally. It is the enablers who prevent the alcoholic's life from spiralling out of control – and in doing so they take away from the alcoholics all responsibility for their own lives and behaviour. In this way, unbeknown to themselves, they maintain the problem.

Very often, the enablers are as sick as the alcoholics

themselves. Both can display obsessive behaviour – the one in trying to get hold of the next drink, and the other trying to stop it! It's no wonder the enablers are often fed-up with the whole situation – and walking out can be a tempting option. Of course, the alcoholics realise this and will often have made contingency plans. That is one of the reasons why many married alcoholics have an extra-marital relationship. They will swear before God that that relationship is the most meaningful ever to them – the one thing that fills the emptiness inside them – but in fact it is just an insurance against being left on their own. Loneliness, though, is a frightening reality for the alcoholics. They will seek company in the strangest of places.

The best advice for those who care for the alcoholics, those who really love them, is to withdraw all support and let them stew. It's a case of being cruel to be kind. That's why it is called 'tough love'. This may seem like betrayal, and is so difficult to do – but sometimes it's the only way forward. The reasoning behind this theory is that it will help the alcoholic to realise his or her true condition and therefore take some remedial action. The longer the enablers offer support, the longer it will take the alcoholic to reach rock bottom. It is only then, hopefully, that suffering – potentially the greatest creative force in nature – will get the alcoholic to change his or her way.

However, whilst this idea is widely accepted, it is very important to be aware of the fact that many alcoholics/addicts will never reach this point because their addiction kills them first – one way or another. As such, it is a calculated risk to withdraw support from the alcoholic in the hope that the seriousness of their predicament will become apparent to them. This is what prevents many loving enablers from letting go of the addict.

Towards the end of my course in Cyncoed College, a survey was conducted into students' leisure interests. I was the only one, apparently, who had no hobbies whatsoever! One of the organisers who analysed the results told me: "Considering your lack of interest in anything extracurricular, Wynford, I reckon you fit the criteria perfectly – you're going to be an alcoholic at the very least!"

Be that as it may, when I really put my mind to something, I could achieve great heights. The next item on my agenda was to find a job – not any job, but a job with the BBC. Nothing else would do! So I immediately began working on a strategy to achieve that aim. The college was very advanced in that it had a television studio and, with the full support of the senior staff, I produced a bilingual television programme on the college closed circuit system. It was a feature programme called *Gyda'r Hwyr* (Evening Time), and the bilingual element was a novelty in broadcasting at the time. It helped, of course, that some of our students were well-known personalities even at that time – people like the singer and entertainer, Dewi Pws, and the greatest name of them all, the international rugby star, Gareth Edwards. An interview with Gareth, especially before an important international match, was bound to be of interest beyond the confines of the college. The BBC heard of the programme and John Roberts Williams, one of the producers of the nightly magazine programme, *Heddiw*, came to see the experiment and was full of praise. The strategy was working!

Shortly afterwards, I had the opportunity to apply for a post with the BBC – that of assistant floor manager – considered to be one of the best ways to get a foot in with the BBC and the television industry, which was in its infancy at the time. There were two posts and 300 applicants, apparently. The interview went like a watch and, of course, one of the posts was mine. I used a technique which is typical of the alcoholic's tendency to try to control other people's minds. When I sat in front of the panel of five men, the sun was right in my eyes. One of them asked if this was bothering me, and when I said it was, three of them jumped up at the same time to close the curtains. I took this as a sign of their eagerness to please me, and that I could control them. By the time they sat down again, my ego had taken over and I thought I was interviewing them! As each one of them asked his question I answered him directly, looking him straight in the eye until he broke the contact. Then I addressed the rest of the group to round off my answer. I did this with each question. Sick, isn't it!

But, as I said, most alcoholics will employ all kinds of 'tricks' to manipulate other people, to get people to do what they want – usually to love them or to respect them. Flattery, lies, bullying, sob stories ... we use them all! That's what I did with the drugs squad in the Top Rank. By the time I'd finished manipulating their minds they were ready to give me a lift home and were almost apologising for daring to suggest that I was taking illegal drugs! I would do the same with doctors, college lecturers, friends, family and neighbours. But if anyone refused to be manipulated by me, then look out! They would be in my bad books forever – and I could be quite mean and resentful! I daren't ask a direct question for fear of receiving a negative response – which I would have interpreted as rejection. As a result, I'm sure there are many people in Wales whom I have ignored, insulted or offended, simply because they were too strong for me to manipulate!

1969 1971

TO BE OR NOT TO BE

Every single day of my sober life I
think of Ronnie Williams – and I
shudder at the thought of what
alcohol can do. I – we – ignore its
insidious power at our peril.

I joined the BBC on July 1st 1969, the same day as the Investiture of the Prince of Wales in Caernarfon Castle. The Investiture evoked strong feelings in the country, but it meant nothing to me one way or the other. I remained outside the fervent nationalistic movement of the time. I couldn't decide whether I was for or against the Investiture – because I had no opinion on anything – so I decided to say nothing, and please everybody!

Mam lent me fifty pounds to tie me over for the first month until my pay came through. Poor thing! Little did she know that I was already deep in debt before I left college and the fifty pounds was a mere spit in the ocean. (My summer job on the buses in Rhyl hadn't made a dent in my debt – nor the £3,000 loan I'd secured from a shady American loan shark!) Mam wanted her money back after my first pay, which was £58. My monthly salary wasn't enough to keep me in food and drink – so the food had to go. I moved to cheaper digs in Pen-y-lan – with an old lady who used to put cotton threads from door to door and up the stairs every time she went out. There's nothing like being trusted!

I was placed in the News Department, together with Iwan Griffiths from Corwen, who had been appointed to the other post, and we worked mostly in the studio in Stacey Road, not far from the BBC Club.

Well, if I was a good drinker before joining the BBC, I was now about to excel in the art! It seemed that everybody in the BBC were drinkers – excessive drinkers. (There must have been some moderate drinkers there but, as a true alcoholic, I chose to drink with the heavyweights.) It's a serious allegation to make, but I'm afraid that there are too many young and talented people, with a tremendous contribution to make to our nation's culture, who have died in ignorance of the effect alcohol had on them at the time. There was one Head of Department who insisted that all members of his department should meet at the BBC Club every Friday lunchtime – to get drunk! And God help those who disobeyed! And after any hard day's work there were nightclubs like the Casino and the Casablanca, and more shady joints in the Docks area, like the North Star, which were regular haunts.

There were some departments within BBC Cymru/Wales that were extremely popular at the time. Light Entertainment was one, under the visionary leadership of Meredydd Evans. The Drama Department too, under D. J. Thomas, was highly respected even amongst the BBC buffs in London and, as is the case today, it was highly productive in both Welsh and English. And that's the department I wanted to work in; that's where my main interest lay. The BBC, however, insisted that I worked in the News and Current Affairs Department, while others, who wanted to work there, were forced to work on drama! There seemed to be a policy of forcing people to work in certain departments against the grain, just to make them conform. Of course, such an attitude was like a red rag to a bull to me! If the BBC wasn't going to yield to my wishes shortly, then I'd have to think of some other strategy – because BBC or not, I was determined to work in drama!

In the meantime I'd fallen head over heels in love! Angela was of Irish descent and was a practising Catholic. One weekend I took her home to Llanllyfni, proud of her, and proud of myself for landing such a beautiful catch; I wanted to show her off to my parents. There was a rather 'uncomfortable' atmosphere in the house all weekend – a feeling of walking on eggshells – but I didn't think for a moment it had anything to do with our visit. On the Sunday morning, however, it all came out. As we were preparing to go to chapel to hear Dad's sermon he took me to one side and said, in a very tense tone of voice: "Wyn. Don't bring that girl to chapel this morning!" He was obviously quite upset, so I asked him: "What's wrong, Dad?" "Look!" he said, "If you bring her to chapel today, I won't be able to preach!" With that he disappeared into the kitchen, slamming the door behind him. And that was that! Angela stayed in the house; Dad gave his sermon as usual; no more was said about it – and I knew better than to ask.

Soon after Angela and I had returned to Cardiff, Arwel came to see me. Yes, he was delivering a message from my parents: that my relationship with Angela had to end. Unbeknown to me, my father harboured a deep prejudice against Catholics; he simply couldn't tolerate them. In addition, Angela's language was English, and that combination was just not on for the younger son of the manse! I tried everything to make them change their minds, but to no avail. And because pleasing Mam and Dad was still my priority in life (although I was living my life in a way that would have broken their hearts had they known the truth), my relationship with Angela had to end. I was too weak to stand up to them at the time, and I was so cross that Arwel had been used to do their dirty work.

What I felt then is known as self-righteous indignation. Over the years thousands of alcoholics have used it as an excuse to drink themselves to death. I didn't manage to kill myself after Angela and I parted so tearfully – but it wasn't for the lack of trying.

By now my physical condition was deteriorating. In addition to the pain in my stomach, my kidneys were beginning to hurt and there was a constant dull pain in my liver, which was a nuisance. I convinced myself that all this was down to playing too much football! I played in goal for Cymry Caerdydd (Cardiff Welsh), which was quite a successful side in the Cardiff League at the time. How I stopped any balls from reaching the back of the net I do not know because, like George Best, I was drunk most of the time; there were far too many players on the field and there were at least two balls coming at me with every shot! So I gave up the football and, indeed, in about a year's time the pain in my kidneys and liver had gone. (Whether it had anything to do with giving up football, I don't know.) However, the pain in my stomach was another matter; it was getting worse and, for some reason, even drinking spirits no longer brought relief. This is when I started thinking I had cancer. Years later I would cry into my beer as I told anyone who would listen that I only had three months to live. I began to arrange my own funeral – right down to the tributes I should receive!

At the time, the programmes I was working on included *Wales Today*, *Week In Week Out*, *Match of the Day* and *Hobby Horse*. *Hobby Horse* was a children's hobbies programme presented by Cliff Morgan and produced by Dewi Griffiths (noted for his international rugby programmes from the Arms Park). I hated working on *Hobby Horse*, not because it was a poor quality programme: quite the opposite, it was an excellent programme broadcast on the network. No, I hated it because the recording took place on Sundays – and each Sunday came after the Saturday night before, and that other awful programme I had to work on, *Match of the Day*!

There were two of us working the floor on *Match of the Day* – Teg (Tecwyn Hughes) as scene boy and me as floor manager. This was a network programme, with contributions from the Cardiff studio, presented by David Parry-Jones. It didn't help the situation that I didn't get on with the presenter. (I wished him good luck once before he presented *Wales Today*. "I don't need any luck from you!" he retorted. The programme didn't go very well for him, and I don't think he refused anybody's 'good luck' after that!) Anyway, the main reason for hating the programme was that it interfered with my drinking. After showing the top games from the London studio, BBC Wales would opt out of the British network to show highlights of games in the Welsh leagues. It meant that we didn't start work on the programme until 9.30 p.m. and usually finished about 11.30 p.m. – which was a bit late to start the drinking session, but it had to happen none the less. Of course, the result was that I was still in a drunken state when I went in to start work on *Hobby Horse* the following morning, and that was a dreadful experience, trying to hide the fact that I was under the influence. Teg and I tried to solve the problem by 'doubling up' – one Saturday I would cover his work on the floor as well as doing mine, and the next Saturday he would cover me – but it didn't work out because by now I needed to drink hard every single day.

Other people drank heavily too; it was part of the BBC

Wales culture at the time – everything seemed to rotate around alcohol. There was one person, though, who stood out – Ronnie Williams – who partnered Ryan Davies in the popular duo, *Ryan a Ronnie*. I watched Ronnie's fall from a top class performer to the depths of alcoholism from a distance. I couldn't bear to be near to him because it worried me – it frightened me, even – but not enough to stop me drinking, either. What happened to Ronnie is the classic story of the alcoholic – a life so full of promise ending in premature death. It's a sad thing to say but the alcoholic can be counted lucky if death comes early. It saves him or her and their loved ones a great deal of pain. Unfortunately, very often, death cannot come early enough to end that pain and they try to take their own lives. Ronnie was successful; I wasn't – that's the only difference between us.

I remember Ronnie Williams as a smart, enthusiastic and extremely talented young man. He, too, had studied at the Welsh College of Music and Drama and he could act, sing, write poetry and he was a very, very humorous scriptwriter. He was an excellent director of programmes, too, and presenting came so naturally to him. In my third year in college, at Cyncoed, I used to visit the 'continuity' studio in Broadway, just to gain some experience of the broadcasting world. It was an interesting way of learning because in 'continuity' you can hear what's going on in different studios, and listen to talkback between the programme directors and the presenters. I was there, with Ronnie Williams, on that historic day in 1968 when Gary Sobers hit six sixes off Malcolm Nash in one over in the game between Notting-hamshire and Glamorgan at St. Helen's. *Grandstand*, a national network programme, was being broadcast live, with David Coleman, one of the slickest and most professional performers I ever heard, presenting the programme in the London studio. The programme switched back and fore between various sports and, in doing so, they missed the historic event at St Helen's. However, the BBC Wales cameras were still recording the cricket at Swansea and we witnessed that amazing feat in the privacy of our small studio in Broadway!

And that's when I also witnessed the brilliance of Ronnie Williams as a TV man. He saw the potential of that historic event and got permission to opt out of the network in order to make a special feature programme about it. At 5.30 that afternoon, viewers to BBC Wales were able to enjoy a fascinating half hour programme that no sports lover would want to miss! It was presented by Ronnie, and he'd also done the directing and the producing – the lot – and it was brilliant!

That evening Ronnie was at the BBC Club in Newport Road. I noticed how unassuming and humble he was in accepting the plaudits for what he had achieved earlier in the afternoon. And I remember thinking to myself, if I'd produced that programme I'd have been blowing my trumpet from the rooftop!

A few years later I was working with him on a BBC production of *The Government Inspector* by Gogol. He was a changed man. He complained that the rehearsals were going on for too long – five minutes after the BBC Club in Llandaf had opened, and he was thirsty! So it was agreed that from then on rehearsals should finish earlier so that Ronnie could get to the bar by opening time. But it wasn't the unprofessional request in itself that stunned me as much as the manner in which it was made. Gone was the endearing humility of 1968 and in its place was an air of arrogance and bumptiousness bordering on the revolting.

From then on his life followed the typical pattern of the alcoholic: moving from one job to another, jumping from one crisis to the next, losing all self-respect and that of his colleagues and family. By the end, bankrupt and hardly able to put two sensible words together, he was suffering from Wernicke-Korsakoff syndrome (also known as 'wet brain') – the sad state when the brain is permanently damaged by alcohol. That is the worst hell of all – the brain like a cabbage but the body refusing to yield to death. I'm sure that Ronnie, though, even in that state, still felt he would be able to drink sensibly one day. Isn't that the insane wish of all alcoholics? The end came with his tragic suicide, the only escape from an illness he didn't realise he had. Or may be he did!

Every single day of my sober life I think of Ronnie Williams – and I shudder at the thought of what alcohol can do. I – we – ignore its insidious power at our peril.

I hadn't been in News and Current Affairs for long before I felt the urge to make a film about my father. It's possible that part of the reason was a subconscious desire to make amends with him for my drinking and for quarrelling with him over Angela. But the main reason was to further my ambition to direct films – an ambition that had been ignited after watching Morris Barry directing *One of the Family*! I wanted to show my superiors what I was capable of, and being a BBC floor manager in Stacey Road was taking me nowhere fast. I was a young man in a hurry. I was convinced

I was going to die of cancer before the age of thirty, so I didn't have much time left to make my mark. And making my mark was very important to me. How else could I justify my existence?

With help from some of my colleagues, I borrowed a camera and some spare film – enough to make a start, anyway – and arranged to visit Gwelfor, the manse, in Llanllyfni. Dad was at his best during the filming. He described his childhood in Dolwyddelan, his stint in the quarry as a young lad, and the experiences that inspired some of his poems. (An anthology of his poems, *Y Ffiol*, (The Goblet) was published after his death.) I think Dad appreciated how I had interpreted his poems. Certainly, his attitude towards me after the filming was very different to what it was before. I had the impression that I'd pleased him. Perhaps he'd realised there was more substance in me than he'd previously given me credit for.

Working on this film was definitely a turning point in the relationship between my father and me. Before then I had been afraid of him, a deferential kind of fear, which meant that the relationship between us was distant and rather cold, without much deep conversation. Soon after we started making the film we became closer as father and son; we began to share our innermost feelings, and he showed a certain respect for my views that I had never experienced before. I felt that his oppressive disappointment in my failings at school was beginning to wane. He even wrote me a poem:

> Danfon i'r llanc dy wynfyd – hedd y doeth,
> O Dduw da, ac iechyd.
> Maddau feiau ei fywyd,
> Arwain ef i'r iawn o hyd.

It's a prayer in which he asks God to give me happiness, peace of mind and good health; to forgive me all my trespasses, and to lead me, always, in the path of righteousness.

It was a fine poem but, to me, it was just empty words – a general sort of poem to fit all occasions and none in particular. At the time, not one of his wishes for me had the slightest chance of being realised. However, without my being aware of it, my father had very cleverly set me specific goals to aim for in the future – goals which I would begin to achieve in years to come; in 1992, to be exact!

When I qualified as a teacher in 1969 my father wrote me a very kind, warm-hearted letter, wishing me well and saying that now I had the means to do whatever I wanted in life. Poor Dad! Far from being free to do what I wanted with my life, I was fast becoming a slave to certain chemicals and a way of life that he would despise. That, too, worried me. I was really afraid of my father finding out the truth.

The film was never finished! (Thanks to Arwel, what was actually filmed is now in safe keeping at the National Library of Wales in Aberystwyth.) But that was typical of me in those days – ready and willing, keen to start any project, but lacking the staying power to complete anything. Stick-to-it-ability eluded me!

Back in Cardiff things were coming to a head. Arwel would often see me staggering home or falling over the chairs in the BBC Club, and he'd ask: "Why do you drink so much, Wyn?" I couldn't answer him. I thought it was the done thing – everybody was drinking! But the truth, of course, was that only a few like me were going over the top. People were talking about me; my drunkenness was a topic of conversation – and a joke. That hurt. I knew that my behaviour was indecent and anti-social but I could do nothing about it. The only thing I could do was to go along with the joke, to take the whole thing lightly. I was just a young lad finding his feet, having a good time, just innocent fun, and so on! But it was no joke really. It's no joke when you can't remember vomiting into your curry; when you shit in your pants and wet your bed.

It was time for me to 'do a geographical', as they say – to move on from Cardiff, away from the mocking mob, and leave behind the bad reputation I was rapidly gaining. If I could get far enough away I could make a fresh start. I wouldn't make the same mistakes again; I wouldn't mix with the same type of people next time. Things would be different. That's what most alcoholics do – they try to run away from their problems. In the Prologue I mentioned my sponsor, Bryn. He typified this behaviour. He went to 33 different countries in six years to try to escape from his problems – without realising that he himself was the problem!

I set my sights on London – with the BBC – and this time I was really going to conquer the world! But all my applications were turned down, and I came to the sad conclusion that the bastards wouldn't be able to recognise true talent if it stared them in their faces! In retrospect, I can see how ridiculously self-opinionated this attitude was – but that's what saved me in the end.

Whilst working on a live programme one day, with people rushing in all directions, as they do at the last minute before going on air, a cameraman bumped into me as he was crossing the floor. "Get out of my bloody way!" he yelled at me. "You're only in this job because of your family connections, anyway!" I was astounded. I knew the BBC had a 'jobs for the boys' reputation, but my appointment had nothing whatsoever to do with 'family connections'. I'd got the job through fair and open competition, and I got it on merit! And this little prick of a cameraman wasn't going to undermine that! Oh, I was so full of self-righteous indignation, and although I didn't say anything to him, the words that crossed my mind were: 'Right! I'll show the bastard!' All alcoholics have said those words at some time, believe you me! That's when sense and reason go out of the window and they are left at the mercy of their selfish and destructive desires.

Although the cameraman's remark was totally unfounded, it triggered a strange reaction in me. In my alcoholic mind I decided that I would prove to the world it wasn't true. I applied for a little-heard-of Welsh Arts Council scholarship to train as a theatre director at the Midlands Arts Centre in Birmingham and the Northcotte Theatre in Exeter. And I got it. That would show the cameraman how wrong he was!

I had been given to understand that I was entitled to a sabbatical year for training purposes. But on the day before I was due to leave Cardiff to begin my training in Birmingham, I was summoned to see my Head of Department, Ken Hawkins, who explained there'd been a mistake – only staff on a higher grade were allowed a sabbatical. He gave me a choice: either to forget the scholarship and remain with the BBC, or to resign from the BBC. Without a second thought – because my head was totally controlled by my self-righteous pride – I resigned there and then.

As I said, that proved to be my salvation. Had I not left then it is certain that I would have ended up as yet another sad statistic on the long list of BBC staff who have died of alcoholism.

I thought of Dad's poem. Perhaps his prayer was being answered!

1971 1972

FATEFUL EVENTS

...My former headmaster had told me
that – that I was deficient and didn't
deserve to succeed. My father, too, and
that lady in the rehearsals in the vestry
in Llansannan all those years ago! ...

The scholarship was only worth a few hundred pounds to cover the whole year – nine months in Birmingham and three in Exeter. So I didn't have much choice but to go for the cheapest digs possible. I landed in a small, damp room in Moseley, Birmingham's poorest area, in a street flanked by a red light area on the one side and a Caribbean ghetto on the other. I'm not a racist, and I wasn't prejudiced in any way – it's just that it was a bit of a culture shock for someone from Llanllyfni in Nantlle Vale!

The first thing I did was to find a GP who would prescribe me sedatives. But I still cried myself to sleep every night, regretting my hasty decision to leave the BBC. Loneliness, too, was a major problem. I didn't have many friends, apart from the few in the local Welsh chapel which I attended. (Keeping up appearances, albeit hypocritically, was so important!) I also frequented the pubs, naturally, to seek companionship. I was mugged one night and had my wallet stolen and my nose broken. In the theatre the following day, my face swollen and bruised, I said I'd tripped and fallen on the pavement. Why I couldn't tell the truth, I don't know. Probably because that would have meant admitting I was drunk at the time, that I was alone, and that I lived in a damp and dirty hovel in the slum area. I couldn't possibly reveal the fragile side of my person. I always wore a mask, figuratively speaking, and the face I put on depended on who I was speaking to, how important they were, and their usefulness to me.

At work, I felt insecure and paranoid. I felt I didn't deserve to be there. Although I'd won the scholarship in fair and open competition I, and only I, knew about the element of duplicity involved. My interview had been a charade, and had the members of the panel dug a little deeper they would have discovered how shallow my qualifications were. My former headmaster had told me that – that I was deficient and didn't deserve to succeed. My father, too, and that lady in the rehearsals in the vestry in Llansannan all those years ago! The dragon inside me was fully roused, relentlessly hissing its negativity: 'You're a no-gooder! You don't deserve to succeed! As a person you are defective!' I was really afraid that Philip Hedley, the director, would discover the truth about me – that I was a fraud.

But I'm in danger of doing myself a disservice here! In an attempt to describe this illness, perhaps I've given the impression that I was hopeless at everything I tried to do. Not at all! For a start, I was an excellent performer. There were some good actors at the Midlands Arts Centre at the time, but I was the best of them all – because I hid all this self-doubt behind a mask of professionalism and enthusiasm that fooled everybody!

Most alcoholics are talented and clever people – they need to be to earn enough money to keep them going and feed their habit! And I was no exception. In fact, alcohol had helped to release my latent talents which had been inhibited, until then, by all kinds of restrictions. It worked wonders when I started drinking, and it still worked for me at this stage – although not as effectively as at first. And that's the sad paradox of the situation. At first the drink, like a good friend, helps the alcoholic to achieve things, but then comes the letdown – a nasty, devastating betrayal. Anyway, as I said, at this stage in my life drink was still a good friend. It still provided me with that all-important 'Wow!' feeling. And, as a trainee theatre director, my talent blossomed. (Of course, at the time, I wasn't aware of the fact that I was a prime example of an alcoholic in denial.)

The Midlands Arts Centre, in Cannon Hill Park, was established by husband and wife team John English and Molly Randele, with the aim of catering for the interests of children and young people. I learned a lot about what should be offered to a young audience and, more importantly perhaps, what should not be offered. The shows, in the main, were all specially commissioned for the company and one thing soon became very clear to me: some writers had the knack of being able to enter the world of children and communicate with them at their own level, whilst others, the majority in fact, couldn't. It's a gift; some people have it, others don't. During my stint in Birmingham I realised that I had been gifted with this rare talent. There had been glimpses of it before, during my teacher training at Cyncoed, but now, at last, there was an opportunity for it to blossom.

At a party in the theatre one night I met a young lady with whom I was to have an 'interesting' encounter. Our friendship quickly developed into a serious relationship, although it was purely platonic. Jemma lived in a wealthy part of the city. Her father was a scrap metal merchant, a multi-millionaire, illiterate, but keen to add a lavish private library to his billiards room.

As it happened, my father had recently been sorting out his study and he had stacks of books to get rid of – ancient theology books and loads of boring autobiographies – all in Welsh, of course. Would these be of any interest to Jemma's father? Certainly! They'd look good on the shelves, and that's all that mattered. He had no intention of learning to read at his age!

Neither did I have any intention of getting engaged to Jemma, but that's what happened at a wild party at the Birmingham BBC Club one night. It was Jemma's idea and, in a drunken state, I agreed wholeheartedly. (I was still in the business of people-pleasing.) The following morning, of course, the idea wasn't so appealing! The first thing that flashed through my mind was, 'What will Mam and Dad say?' Engagement, in those days, more so than today, was a serious affair with the two families coming together and announcements in the local papers and so on. It was an important step in life and certainly not one to be taken lightly.

It was only natural, then, that Jemma wanted to meet my parents. God help me! That could not be allowed to happen – my mother would drop dead! Let me explain. Jemma was a blonde bombshell whose language and manner were more suited to being a hostess at a seedy Soho nightclub than the daughter-in-law of the manse in Llanllyfni! But I was being swept along by a huge wave, with Jemma and her father openly planning the grandest wedding Birmingham had ever witnessed. I found it impossible to say 'No!' or do anything to pull out of the absurd contract. My most immediate fear was that Jemma's father would mention the engagement to my father as they negotiated the purchase of the books for his wretched library on the telephone. Had that happened I think I would have contemplated suicide!

Two things happened that saved my life. Firstly, as I was going through my sob story one night in the BBC Club, Islwyn Maelor Evans and his wife, Jean, said I could stay with them. Secondly, Wilbert Lloyd Roberts, Artistic Director of the Welsh-language section of the Wales Theatre Company, invited me to direct the performance of the play commissioned for the Bangor and District National Eisteddfod in August 1971.

Islwyn and Jean worked with the BBC in Birmingham. Their kind offer was attractive in two ways: firstly, I'd be able to turn my back on the damp and lonely room in Moseley and, even more importantly, their home was on the other side of town – out of Jemma's sight, and out of reach, once I'd plucked up the courage to call the engagement off! It didn't take me long to accept! I stayed with them for a short while only, but during that time they proved to be two of the best friends I ever had. In the end it was Jemma who called the engagement off. (Alcoholics find it so hard to say 'No' to anyone.) Somehow she must have realised what was in store for her, and I thank God for that!

As I travelled on the train to Bangor I was full of excitement at the prospect of directing *Rhyfedd y'n Gwnaed* (How Strangely We Are Made), a trilogy of short plays by one of Wales' foremost playwrights, John Gwilym Jones. At last, here was the opportunity I'd been waiting for to make my mark in the world of the theatre. Working alongside one of my idols, Wilbert Lloyd Roberts, and doing my bit for the Wales Theatre Company. It was a dream come true. Wasn't this the very reason I'd gone to Drama College in the first place? And this could be the very occasion to enable me to turn my back on my evil past and begin a new and exciting chapter in my life. I knew I had to control my drinking, hide the fact – or even give it up, perhaps. And to top it all, I could stay with my parents; they'd be so proud of me – guest director of the commissioned play at the National Eisteddfod – the return of the prodigal son, no less! 'Bangor, here I come!'

Whilst working on *Rhyfedd y'n Gwnaed*, I learned a great deal about the art of producing plays, not least the high level of 'man management' skills required! The project, as a whole, was very successful but I must admit that one of the actors proved to be very difficult to handle. His negative and uncooperative response triggered the latent self-deprecation element in me and I soon forgot the vows I made on the train as I sought solace in the nearest pub.

However, the most important thing that happened during that time was that I met Meira again. She was living with her parents in Y Fron, better known as Upper Llandwrog, a small village near the coast a few miles south of Caernarfon. We had attended the same secondary school and we had actually sung duets in many a local *eisteddfod* – but much water had gone under the bridge since then! One sunny Sunday afternoon, during a break in rehearsals, I went to the beach at Dinas Dinlle, my favourite place in the whole world. And there, amongst the hundreds of visitors, I just happened to bump into Meira who was there with her family and a boyfriend. We had a brief chat – I mentioned the work I was doing at the time and invited her to the rehearsals, if she was interested – and then I went on my way.

One night, soon after that chance meeting, Meira rang me at Gwelfor. She wanted to come to the rehearsals. I was a little surprised (I hadn't given the invitation a second thought, really) but, I must admit, I was more than a little excited! That phone-call proved to be fateful. From then on our relationship blossomed into a love so deep, so strong, that it would overcome all the trials that lay ahead. Meira wasn't aware at the time that I was an alcoholic, and I managed to hide the fact from her for some time. Whether knowing would have made any difference, I don't know. But what I do know is that because of my alcoholism, because of the way she has handled the whole situation, Meira is loved and revered by everyone. Needless to say, my name is at the top of that list.

Immediately after the Eisteddfod I began my stint at the Northcott Theatre in Exeter. I found myself cheap accommodation and a doctor to provide me with my necessary drugs and then I set about tasting the local beverage, scrumpy. The condition of my stomach had deteriorated during my stay in North Wales, but it was about to get much worse!

Throughout my period in Exeter, I was burning with ambition to make a name for myself in the theatre world. Emboldened with alcohol-fuelled courage, I contacted Jean-Louis Barrault, the famous French actor, director and mime artist. I was full of admiration for him, and was particularly interested in his mime work. There were great possibilities to develop Welsh theatre in that medium, I thought. Barrault had been recently sacked as artistic director of Théâtre de France because of his support for the student rebellion there in 1968, when he'd offered them shelter in the theatre. When I got in touch with him he was on his way to London, with his actress wife, Madeleine Renauld, to direct his controversial production of *Rabelais* at The Old Vic. He was gracious enough to meet me to discuss my ideas and agreed to 'take me under his wing' for a period in France – if I could secure further funding from the Welsh Arts Council.

That application was flatly rejected. I was told to return to Wales, as it was payback time! The timing was fortuitous. *Rhyfedd y'n Gwnaed*, the play I had directed at the National Eisteddfod the previous August, was due to do an all-Wales tour – and I was invited to direct it. After that, I might still have pursued my dream of working with Jean-Louis Barrault had it not been for my father's untimely death, which shook me to the core.

My father had been behaving oddly for some time – walking into the house next door instead of ours, for example, and driving the wrong way around a roundabout on the way to visit Rowenna and Rheinallt, my brother-in-law, in Anglesey. Thinking it was something to do with his eyesight, he made an appointment with the optician. It turned out that he was, indeed, blind on the left side – but the cause of his blindness was eventually diagnosed as a tumour on the brain. He was taken to Walton Hospital, Liverpool, where he had an emergency operation. It was successful, and he recovered – for a while.

For some strange reason Rowenna, Arwel and I decided not to tell my father or my mother the real facts about Dad's condition. It was farcical, really, because both of them knew what the score was – he had cancer of the lungs with secondary growth on the brain. The modern hospital policy of openness and frankness is much more acceptable. After all, it's the individual's privilege to have the opportunity to come to terms with his own death.

I can't resist the temptation to draw a parallel between how we decided to treat my father's illness and how families often treat alcoholism – with denial – and that can be just as ridiculous and harmful as what we were trying to do with my father's illness. We were walking on eggshells and avoiding the truth. Dad's cancer was like a huge pink elephant right in the centre of our lives – but not one of us talked about it. No one talks about alcoholism, either. Instead, many families wrap the alcoholics in cotton wool to avoid giving them an excuse to drink more; they pretend that everything is hunky-dory and won't allow anybody in on the secret, not even someone who might be able to help. 'There's nothing wrong with our family,' is their mantra.

Could it be that this response is due to a feeling of embarrassment and shame? Certainly, there is a social stigma attached to alcoholism, and that is not at all helpful. If a person collapses in the street with a heart attack, everyone rushes to offer help. But if an alcoholic collapses in a heap he is treated with disdain. The general perception is that the heart attack is not the person's fault, whereas in the case of the alcoholic, it's entirely his own fault! In fact, nothing could be further from the truth! The number of heart attacks in this country could be drastically reduced, we are informed, if people ate a healthier diet, stopped smoking and exercised more. With alcoholics, the general attitude is: 'Well if he didn't drink so much, he wouldn't be in that mess!' I'm not belittling the difficulty of giving up smoking, for example, but people in general have absolutely no idea how difficult it is for an alcoholic to stop drinking. There's a lack of understanding, and therefore a lack of sympathy. It might help society if it were able to see alcoholism as a disease and not as a disgrace.

Western civilisation feels threatened by Al-Qaeda-type

terrorism. But the greatest threat to our civilisation is from within our own society – addiction to alcohol and other drugs and all the related illnesses. Unless we change our attitude to this problem, the future of our civilisation is increasingly bleak.

However, there are two known facts about alcoholism. Firstly, before they can begin the process of recovery, alcoholics must accept the facts as they are – that they are alcoholics. Secondly, the decision to take the first step to recovery must be theirs, and theirs alone. Once that decision has been made, obviously, there is need for constant support, but most important of all, I believe, is the acceptance of a 'higher power' that will provide the necessary strength to succeed. The individual must feel 'empowered' – strong in the faith that recovery is, indeed, possible to achieve.

For those who know their Bible, faith, of course, is the power that makes anything possible – even 'move mountains', figuratively speaking! I believe that the alcoholics' recovery programme is based on the same principle. Faith is not necessarily a religious phenomenon – but it is a belief in a power that is greater than ourselves, beyond us and yet within our grasp, constantly there when we need it. When this mental state has been achieved, mountains can be moved! I've seen people conquering untreatable cancer through this process. Surely, this provides hope for the alcoholic – and, I believe, for all the ills of our society.

But I digress. Dad came home from Walton Hospital a new man. His eyesight was normal and he got stuck into editing the final proofs of his anthology of poems, *Y Ffiol*. Six weeks later, however, he took a sudden turn for the worse.

On that very day Sionyn, Dad's dog, ran in front of a car in the street outside the house and was killed instantly. Sionyn had a very close affinity with Dad and I'm sure he had a premonition of my father's impending death. When the end came Dad was being comforted by a fellow minister, the Rev. John Roberts of Moriah, Caernarfon. They exchanged expressions of faith and my father died as strong as ever in his religious conviction.

The death of the Rev. Robert Owen, Llanllyfni, was a great loss to us as a family and to the whole community. On the 8th of March 1972, his remains were cremated at Colwyn Bay Crematorium. I could not grieve properly. That gift had been stolen from me by sedatives and alcohol. My senses were dulled, my feelings numbed. It was not until 1992 that I was able to grieve properly for my father, and 1993 before I was able to begin to love him as I do today.

Mam had to leave the manse after six months, which is normal procedure for ministers' widows. Fortunately, Rowenna and Arwel were able to buy her a bungalow in Llanfairpwllgwyngyll, Anglesey, and that's where I lived, too, until I got married.

During this period I had been touring with the Wales Theatre Company's pantomime, *Mawredd Mawr!* (Goodness Gracious!). I played the part of ugly fairy Fferi Nuff (a play on the words 'fairy' and 'fair enough'). It was a small part in the script, but I was on stage most of the time, responding to everything that went on, and that's where the humour lies every time – in the response! As I mentioned before, I knew I had the talent to communicate with children, to enter their world, and I transformed Fferi Nuff to be the star of the show

– much to the annoyance of some of the other, more important characters, who were clearly jealous! In fact, I gained quite a reputation for ad-libbing on stage; it often stretched the tolerance of the other performers to almost breaking point but it never failed to generate a good response from the audience – a fact that didn't go unnoticed by the 'people that mattered' in the Wales Theatre Company hierarchy.

Meira was a great source of strength to me at this time. When she was with me I could control my drinking to some extent. But once I was away on tour I was hopeless and I was drunk most of the time. The pain in my stomach was, by now, excruciating; alcohol was the only thing that offered any kind of relief. By the morning after, of course, I was back to square one and had to go on the mad merry-go-round once again – the merry-go-round that ensured my general behaviour was equally mad.

I was barred from the Fishguard Bay Hotel once for destructive conduct. The whole pantomime crew was staying there and one evening, in a drunken stupor, I insulted and offended one of them and he went to his room in a huff. I later decided to apologise, so I went to look for him. He wouldn't open the door, so I kicked it open – only to find it was the wrong room, a lady's room at that! I ran up to the next floor and tried another room. Still no answer, so I did the same again – smashed the door down in my temper. I never found the right room!

My profuse apologies the next day were not accepted. I was barred from that hotel and, as a measure of internal discipline, I was also barred from staying in the same hotel as the rest of the crew in Swansea, the pantomime's next port of call.

During my time with the Wales Theatre Company I had become very friendly with another actor, Mici Plwm. We developed a close rapport both on and off stage, and that inevitably meant we were partners in drink, too. We drank during every performance – we had a glass of vodka waiting for us in the wings after each stage appearance. The trick was to stay just about sober enough to complete the show but, by the end, we'd be well away. And in the wild parties in the hotels after the shows, I'd often make a fool of myself. This is the time I switched from vodka to brandy. During one of the shows someone had spilled the vodka that was waiting for Mici Plwm and me in the wings and it had burned the varnish on the chair right down to the bare wood. "Good God!" Mici said, "If that's the effect it has on the chair, what the hell does it do to our stomachs?" I suggested we should drink brandy instead – and that's what we did for the rest of the tour!

Despite my heavy drinking and all the stunts and unruly behaviour, someone in the hierarchy still believed I had the potential to make a significant contribution to the theatre in Wales. I was invited by Wilbert Lloyd Roberts to lead an innovative and exciting project called *Y Theatr Ifanc* (The Young Theatre), with the specific aim of attracting young actors to join the profession.

At that time the future of the theatre in Wales was uncertain, mainly due to a dearth of professional actors. There were plenty of amateur actors, and even part-time professional actors, but few were prepared to take the plunge, as it were, into the insecure world of professional acting. A national theatre could not possibly thrive on that basis. This recruiting exercise, then, was an important development and

I was proud to have been selected to be in charge.

'Why me?' I thought. Well, it must be an acknowledgement of my performing talent but, also, of the ability I had displayed to communicate with young people. My ego had received a terrific boost, and the doubting dragon inside me had to hold her fire! Could this be my opportunity to make a real name for myself – to be 'somebody' at last?

The colleges of Wales were all actively involved in amateur drama productions, and that seemed an obvious place to start. I decided to target students in their second year, because by their third and final year students are more tuned in to the attractions of a secure career path – or they were, in those days! If I could give second-year students an enjoyable and positive experience of acting, it might encourage them to make a go of it as a career – as full-time professionals.

So, I visited all the colleges and selected twenty-five students to take part in the venture. I targeted the National Eisteddfod at Haverfordwest in August 1972 for the first performance, and the play I had in mind was *Y Rhai a Lwydda* (The Ones Who Will Succeed) by the late Bernard Evans. He was a producer in the Schools Department at the BBC in Cardiff at the time, and this play was based on the emergence of unionism in Wales in the Nineteenth Century, in the days when William Crawshay was king of the iron industry in Merthyr, and Dic Penderyn was executed in Cardiff jail after being wrongly accused of stabbing a soldier during the famous Merthyr Uprising of 1831 – a theme to appeal to all young people everywhere!

The performances at Haverfordwest were well received and there followed a short tour of the theatres around Wales.

The project proved to be a great success. A group of promising young actors had been enthused by the experience and were seriously considering a future in the acting profession. (Indeed, it turned out that the vast majority of that group later became professional actors or production technicians.)

At the end of the tour I was asked by the Welsh Arts Council to prepare a report on the project and to suggest a way forward for The Young Theatre. I proposed that it should be established on a permanent footing and developed independently of the Wales Theatre Company. Some people might regard this as an attempt to create a niche for myself, since I would obviously be in a strong position to be appointed as director! But I genuinely believed that the theatre in Wales would benefit from a diversity of artistic policy – free from the dictatorship of Wilbert Lloyd Roberts, Director of the Wales Theatre Company, which I saw as a growing problem. Despite his undoubted ability, Wilbert would not delegate any responsibility to anyone and I regarded this as a threat to the whole future of the Company since no one was being groomed to succeed him. (In retrospect I fully appreciate that I wouldn't – or shouldn't – have been considered for the post anyway since I was so undependable. But there were others in the ranks of the Wales Theatre Company at the time who had a great contribution to make.)

When I presented the report to one of the officers of the Arts Council, in the autumn of 1972, it was thrown back in my face – literally! To me, the rejection of that proposal was a clear sign of the underlying tensions that existed in the theatre world in Wales at the time. It was also the end of another pipe dream!

1972 1978

DEAD AND FAMOUS AT THIRTY?

... I would have killed myself before
then had I not been so afraid of
dying. That was ironic – being
afraid to die and yet causing my
own slow death with alcohol!

Towards the end of 1972 my career took a new turn. I was invited by Dr. Meredydd Evans, Head of the BBC Light Entertainment Department, to join the team which was to present a new programme called *Teliffant*, a hilariously mad Welsh-language children's programme, which was his brainchild. Whilst continuing to do work for the Welsh-language section of the Wales Theatre Company, much of my time for the next few years was devoted to *Teliffant*, which was based at the BBC in Cardiff. (For a time I also presented a children's quiz programme for HTV, the independent TV company based in Cardiff, but the pressure of work was too great and after three series I had to give that up.) The basic idea behind *Teliffant* was that I should take the camera crew to track down a weird creature called Teliffant which lived in the hills around Lake Bala. At first the programme had a very loose format, not much more than a vehicle for various sketches, knock-knock jokes and jokes sent in by child viewers, presented by actors in the studio. My first contribution was on film since I was still working on the pantomime at the time, but then I joined the other actors in the studio in Cardiff.

I soon came to the conclusion that the programme's format needed to be radically changed. In its current format it didn't utilise the actors' talents – any decent presenter could have done the job equally well. I wanted something more demanding, more exciting! There were no children's sit-com programmes in Welsh at the time, and I thought *Teliffant* had great potential to fill that gap. Unfortunately, no one else agreed with me. The two producers, Rhydderch Jones and Bryn Richards, were adamant that it should stay as it was.

And so began a personal battle – a battle which I was determined to win.

Alcoholics are often accused of being weak-willed. How often do we hear the words: 'If they had a bit more will power they could easily stop drinking!' Not so! Alcoholics can be the most strong-willed and stubborn of all people. In my case, for example, I would take a few gulps of whisky first thing in the morning – and throw up immediately. Then I'd drink some more, and throw up again ... and more and more until it eventually stayed down. Then I could drink all day long. Now that's what I call will power! And I had it in abundance, as Rhydderch Jones and Bryn Richards were to find out. Yes, I won the battle in the end, as I knew I would, and *Teliffant* became a popular sit-com programme with an inimitable set of characters – Oli Olwyn (Oli the Wheel) played by Olwen Rees, Myff Taglog played by Myfanwy Talog, Plwmsan y Twmffat Twp (Plwmsan the Pear-shaped Dunce) played by Mici Plwm, and Syr Wynff ap Concord y Bos (Sir Wynff son of Concorde, the Boss) played by myself – with the name being an obvious reference to the shape of my nose!

Teliffant was recorded at the new BBC studios in Llandaf, Cardiff, on Saturdays. Early on the Wednesday morning each week I used to travel down from Llanfairpwll-gwyngyll, Anglesey, where I lived with my mother, and spend the rest of the week rehearsing. I was at my best in the morning – because in the afternoon I'd be drunk. I was told recently that people were afraid to work with me after lunch – that I'd change from being a fairly pleasant person in the morning into a critical, self-opinionated tyrant in the afternoon. I'd go to the BBC Club for a liquid lunch of vodka and beer, and always took some vodka back with me for the afternoon session. I must have been a thoroughly obnoxious person; I can't imagine how the cast and crew put up with me.

Neither can I understand how I wasn't arrested for drink driving. On the Saturday night, if I could muster enough desire to begin the journey home, I'd always have a quarter bottle of vodka or whisky by my side in the passenger seat. I was stopped by the police, once, on the outskirts of Cardiff. It was at the time of the oil crisis of 1973 when Prime Minister Edward Heath had imposed a three-day working week and a speed limit of 50 mph in order to save fuel. I'd been speeding, of course, but I expected to be arrested for being drunk at the wheel, not for speeding. After being cautioned about observing the speed limit, one of the officers pointed to the half empty bottle of whisky on the passenger seat and said, with a wry smile: "And I wouldn't drink any more of that stuff, either, if I were you, mate. Off you go!" And so I was allowed to continue my dangerous drive to North Wales. The drink-drive law never deterred me from driving under the influence of alcohol. When it came down to a choice between drinking and driving, nine times out of ten I did both! It's impossible to legislate against an illness that defies all logic.

On the 23rd of April 1973, Meira and I were married at a small chapel, Cesarea, in the village of Upper Llandwrog, where she was a member. It was a newsworthy occasion and HTV was present to film the proceedings. We headed for Bodfach Hall in Llanfyllin for the first night of our honeymoon but on arrival we were waylaid by members of the Bala branch of Merched y Wawr (the Welsh equivalent of the WI) who recognised me as Fferi Nuff and the chap who presented the HTV quiz. It was gratifying, of course, to be recognised in that way but by the time we got away Meira was deadbeat and fell asleep straight away! As I sipped champagne beside the sleeping beauty I made a promise that things would be different from then on.

In two days' time I was back in Cardiff, recording another episode of *Teliffant*. Times were pretty tough financially. It's not easy for actors to make a living, especially those in the Welsh medium and, contrary to popular belief, actors don't get paid all that well anyway. The majority of any programme's funding goes into the technology and post-production aspects. In my case, certainly, I would not have been able to continue with my acting career were it not for the fact that Meira had a steady income as a teacher.

In the same year, 1973, I accepted an invitation from the National Eisteddfod of Wales to produce a review show for the Eisteddfod at Rhuthun. I went to see two of my favourite comedy scriptwriters, Dafydd Glyn Jones and Bruce Griffiths – both of whom are also eminent university academics and co-editors of The Welsh Academy English-Welsh Dictionary. We soon agreed on a theme and a title for the review – *Jiwbili Jiwbilant, Agent Eithriadol a Dienyddiwr Swyddogol yr Hen Gorff* (Jubilant Jubilee, Agent Extraordinaire and Official Executioner of the Calvinistic Methodists). Geraint Jarman, a popular Welsh singer, helped us with the lyrics and the music. The title itself encapsulated the theme, which was about a mad Methodist preacher called Jiwbili Jiwbilant who had returned from America on a mission to save the traditional (dry) Welsh Sunday from going the way of the Continental Sunday!

On the day of the performance, in Denbigh Town Hall, there was an incident that almost ruined the production – and my career! After a break in the final rehearsal the cast and production crew returned to the hall to be greeted by the fire brigade. The heat from one of the lights had apparently caused the stage curtain to catch fire and had it not been for the quick thinking of a member of the public, it seems the town hall would have been razed to the ground that day. We managed to salvage the curtain, however, and the performance that evening was a notable success. Some time later the National Eisteddfod tried to sue me for thousands of pounds in compensation for replacing the burnt curtain. Luckily, I was able to prove that the curtain had not been made fire-resistant, as was required by law. But it seemed the National Eisteddfod had it in for me: within a year they were at it again, threatening to bankrupt me!

While all this was going on in my professional career, there were certain developments in my private life, too. I had continued to attend chapel regularly – traditions die hard in Wales, and anyway, I owed that much to my father's memory. It was no surprise, then, that I was nominated to become a deacon at Fron chapel. Why should it have been a surprise? I, personally, was aware of the hypocrisy of the situation, but no one else in the neighbourhood knew of my 'other' life! There was a strange battle going on in my head; despite my worsening alcoholism, I still had an awareness of right and wrong. I still had a conscience. Too much conscience, in fact, because that's what caused the feelings of guilt and shame that plagued me so much. So I drank in order to overcome those feelings; I drank myself into oblivion. What a crazy

Catch 22 situation!

I had no choice but to accept the nomination, really. First of all, a refusal would have required an explanation, and that was out of the question! Secondly, I couldn't disappoint my mother who was so proud that I'd been nominated. I couldn't bring myself to tell her: 'Look, Mam, I'm not the kind of person you think I am! I don't even believe in God!' (I remember raising doubts with my father, once, about the existence of God. He gave me a hell of a row, saying: "You believe in our God and that's the end of the matter, Jac-y-do!") But the strange thing is that, deep down in my soul, I wanted to believe in God. I also wanted people to look up to me. I craved for people to respect me – as they would a deacon. I was totally lacking in self-esteem; I knew the condition was self-inflicted, and yet I was clutching at anything that could restore even a tiny amount of it.

So, at a meeting of the Arfon Presbytery in Tal-y-sarn chapel, I was ordained a deacon. In my acceptance speech I referred to the poem which my father had dedicated to me and in which he had implored God to forgive me all my trespasses, and to lead me, always, in the path of righteousness. I didn't specify any trespasses! Nor did I mention my 'faith' – or lack of it. My private life and innermost thoughts remained top secret! But, as the saying goes, 'Truth will out!' and as time went by, more and more people discovered the true Wynford Owen. I remained a deacon, though, still clinging on to a semblance of respectability.

After the altercation with the National Eisteddfod committee regarding the fire damage at Denbigh Town Hall in 1973, I didn't expect any further offers of work from that direction. But, surprise, surprise, out of the blue came an invitation to direct the musical show at the Carmarthen Eisteddfod in 1974. *Nia Ben Aur* (Nia of the Golden Locks), a theme with its roots in Celtic mythology, would be the first ever Welsh-language rock opera, and the offer to direct it was an honour and a challenge – both of which I couldn't resist!

Welsh pop music was going through a purple patch at the time. Individual artistes who made a name for themselves during that period included Endaf Emlyn, Meic Stevens, Dafydd Iwan, Mary Hopkins, Heather Jones and Huw Jones, and there were several groups that were in great demand throughout Wales, such as Sidan, Hergest, Y Tebot Piws and Ac Eraill, to name but a few. The music and the lyrics for the rock opera were composed by members of the Ac Eraill group. They had already released the main song, 'Nia Ben Aur', as a single and it had really caught the public imagination. There was great expectancy, therefore, surrounding the performance of the rock opera *Nia Ben Aur* in the grand pavilion of the National Eisteddfod at Carmarthen in August 1974.

At the first meeting of the organising committee, I commended the members on their bold and adventurous decision to give the young generation such a golden opportunity to display their talent – a feature that had been so obviously missing until then. It soon became evident, however, that the Drama Committee had not fully realised the nature or the scale of what they had commissioned. This was no traditional, run-of-the-mill concert! This was a fully-fledged, professionally directed musical show with singers, actors, dancers, a narrator, an orchestra, and a lighting and sound system worth thousands of pounds. On top of all that there would be a set and costumes, and substantial rehearsal time at a venue in Cardiff. Although many of the performers and musicians would be amateur, at least thirty would be professional, and the choreographers and technicians would all have to be professional. Put bluntly, the show had not been properly costed or budgeted. There was no way the show could be staged.

It was Wilbert Lloyd Roberts, Director of the Wales Theatre Company, who came to our rescue. He offered me all of the technical resources and the services of all the technicians free of charge! This was a tremendous boost and it meant that the costings of the rest of the show were more or less within the available budget. My bank manager, however, wasn't happy at all! Wise man as he was, he insisted on a clause being inserted in my contract absolving me from any personal liability should the cost of the show exceed the proposed budget. Thank God for bank managers! Otherwise, the Eisteddfod Committee would have succeeded in making me bankrupt.

All the preparations went well. Towards the end members of the public came in droves to marvel at the singing and the choreography in the rehearsals at the Urdd Centre in Conway Road, Cardiff, and there was a general feeling abroad that *Nia Ben Aur* was going to be a super show. The only problem was that the narrator, Gruffudd Miles, a known alcoholic, was drinking too much and becoming unreliable; he was in grave danger of losing his voice completely by the night of the performance. As for my own drink problem, I managed to be very discreet. I'd sneak out of the rehearsal room every now and then to have a quick swig of vodka – downing a quarter bottle in an afternoon – but no one noticed. Gruff, on the other hand, was unable to do that. In fact, he had reached rock bottom and there was nothing he could do to control it.

When we got to the Eisteddfod ground on the day of the show, however, things began to disintegrate. First of all the early evening concert had over-run and we had to do a lot of clearing up before we could begin to build our set on the stage. Then there was Gruff – his voice croaking and almost gone – and I, personally, took charge of making sure he didn't drink any more. (Set a poacher ... ! I knew all his devious tricks before he even thought of them!) But the main problem on the night, and it turned out to be disastrous, was a fault with the sound system.

State-of-the-art radio mikes had been hired for the performance. They were expensive, and had to have a special licence from the Post Office because of their potential to interfere with police and ambulance messages – but they were essential for the show to be effective in such a huge pavilion. However, for some unknown reason, as the show progressed these mikes went down one by one – and the show was ruined! There I was, sat in the front row with Wilbert Lloyd Roberts and Gray Evans, my assistant director, completely gob-smacked and unable to do a thing about it.

That must rank with one of the saddest experiences of my life, to see such a beautiful creation disintegrating before my very eyes. The disappointment of that night scarred me for years; to say that it marred my career development is an understatement. It took a long time to get over the disaster of the first, and last, performance of *Nia Ben Aur*. In fact, I was twelve years into my recovery before I began to feel the urge to be involved with producing and directing again. Of course, that kind of reaction is typical of the alcoholic – they dwell on any negative experiences and turn them into an excuse to shut the door on any new opportunities.

Despite the failure of the sound system on the night, that production of *Nia Ben Aur* proved to be an acknowledged landmark in the development of musical theatre in Wales. It was the dawn of a new 'professionalism' in such productions and it ushered in a new generation of performers such as Caryl Parry Jones, Clive Harpwood, Dewi Pws and Hefin Elis – all of whom went on to become household names in the Welsh music scene. Anyway, not unexpectedly, that production of *Nia Ben Aur* exceeded its budget by a few thousand pounds. And to compound the devastating disappointment of the actual event, the Eisteddfod Committee tried to sue me for the loss! My own personal debt at the time was pretty horrendous and there's no doubt that I would have become bankrupt had it not been for that 'no liability' clause which my bank manager had insisted on putting in my contract. Looking back, I can accept much of the responsibility for the overspending, but at the time I had the impression that I was being made the scapegoat, and I held a grudge against the Eisteddfod, as an institution, for years.

Soon afterwards, I was admitted to the C&A Hospital in Bangor to treat a massive duodenal ulcer, caused by all the pressures and strains I was under at that time. That's the reason I gave – it had nothing at all to do with my drinking habits and all the tablets I was taking – and people believed me! I'd lost a tremendous amount of weight and looked like a skeleton. Meira, poor thing, had to look on helplessly as I continued to torture my body and destroy my health. For a time she really believed she could change things, and stop me drinking altogether! Sadly, most partners of alcoholics suffer this delusion. I regarded her attempts to help me as 'nagging', which gave me an added excuse to continue drinking! Events then followed a typical pattern; rather than accept the fact that she couldn't do anything about it, she began to convince herself that my drinking wasn't all that excessive anyway, that I was exhausted, not drunk, and wasn't it normal for all men to get drunk occasionally? This was the ultimate 'denial'! Not only was I convincing myself there was nothing wrong with me, but now Meira was supporting me in that view. Bingo! And that's a common scenario with alcoholics, their partners and their families – they paper over all the cracks with the usual mantra: 'There's nothing wrong with our family!' as they try to maintain a façade of normality. That's the only way they can cope with the situation.

I was ill for quite a while after the operation. The pain in my stomach was still there and I was prescribed stronger painkillers. My GP advised me to take a little tonic – and suggested a bottle of Guinness or Mackeson Stout a day! His advice was gladly taken but, unfortunately, rather too enthusiastically! Within a fortnight the daily dose had risen to ten or more bottles. I also started brewing my own beer – as a hobby – just something to pass the time while I was recuperating!

It was during this time at home that I heard of the death of Gruff Miles who was the narrator in *Nia Ben Aur*. I don't know to what extent alcohol played a part in the horrific accident that killed him and a friend but I'd been half expecting news of his death because it just wasn't possible for him to survive for much longer. It did cross my mind that such an accident could easily have happened to me but, for some reason, it didn't register that what contributed to his death was also taking a grip on me, too.

By this time my financial situation was pretty grave and I was desperate to find some sort of employment. Salvation came in the form of the well-known author and journalist, T. Glynne Davies. He'd been presenter of the BBC daily news programme, *Bore Da* (Good Morning), and had just been promoted to the post of editor. He invited me to present the programme for three days, Monday to Wednesday, and for the rest of the week I'd be rehearsing and recording *Teliffant* in Cardiff. T. Glynne and I were close friends – both of us were rather too fond of drink – and we used to meet in the Union pub on the banks of the Menai Straits every lunchtime for some relaxation after a hard morning's work.

At first I really enjoyed presenting the programme, but getting up at 4.00 o'clock every morning played havoc with my stomach. I couldn't eat anything before the programme, as I was a bundle of nerves, and the fact that it was a live broadcast added tremendously to the stress. Waking up in the morning was a problem since I went to bed every night hopelessly drunk and under the influence of the strong sedatives, which I swallowed like Smarties. It wasn't long before this misuse of alcohol and drugs began to have an effect on my speech. It began with a slight stutter and now and again I'd fail to pronounce a certain word. Nothing too serious – I just had to concentrate very hard, that's all. It soon deteriorated, though, and I was unable to utter some words without holding my chin in both hands and twisting my face to get the words out. It sounded like a slowed-down tape recording. Then came the final straw – the return of my dyslexia. I completely failed to read one story, the words dancing around in front of my eyes, and my confidence was shattered. That was the end of my career as a news presenter.

As my life began to spiral out of control I was hit by yet another crisis. The Inland Revenue had changed their policy on expenses allowances and, after a prolonged inquiry, they decided that I owed them £6,000 in tax. Six thousand pounds was a huge sum of money at the time – the house we had bought in Bontnewydd near Caernarfon, was only seven and a half – and I had to borrow the money from the bank to pay the tax bill.

In a desperate attempt to get me to get a grip on my life, and to behave more responsibly, Meira suggested that we should start a family. The idea appealed to me – it might provide me with another distraction from the pain of living – but the way things were going for me at the time, with the whole world conspiring against me, I didn't think there was much chance of success! And as I blundered on from one crisis to the next, it never occurred to me that my failures had anything to do with my own weaknesses. It was always someone else's fault – Meira for nagging so much, the BBC for not giving me more work, the Bank Manager ... etc. etc. I really thought I could stop drinking if only all these things could be put right! I was also being eaten up with jealousy – everything seemed to work out all right for other people. I began to covet what other people possessed – their success, their ability to make friends, their wives! I compared myself with other people and always came out second best. The old dragon inside me was still breathing fire.

Very few people were welcome at our home. I didn't trust anyone. The less people knew about us, the less damage they could do to us. You can only be on good terms with others if you are on good terms with yourself. That's a fact, and since I hated myself, intensely, my relationship with everyone else, too, was based on hatred. I hadn't kept in touch with anyone from Llansannan or Llanllyfni, or with anyone from school or college. All links with my past had been allowed to wither away, partly due to being ashamed of myself but also because I didn't feel that I belonged to anyone or to any place. I didn't support any football team; wasn't involved with any political party and wasn't a member of any society or club – only the chapel, and that was barefaced hypocrisy. I even kept members of the family at arm's length. By now Arwel and Margaret were living in Creigiau near Cardiff and had four children. Arwel had a good job as editor of the Welsh-language TV magazine programme, *Heddiw* (Today). I used to stay with them now and again, but the relationship was quite distant, really. The same was true of Rowenna and Rheinallt and their two children who lived in Llanfairpwll-gwyngyll. There was the occasional visit and an invitation to tea on Christmas day, but nothing more. Even if I'd wanted to, I couldn't allow myself to get too close to them because I had too many secrets, too many things to hide from them. Mam was more of a problem. I felt, somehow, that she knew what was going on but that she didn't want to admit it to herself, and she avoided the issue by talking incessantly about anything and everything – everything but the truth. I just let her carry on, agreeing with everything she said. By now I felt under siege; it was a case of me against the whole world. No! Correction! Me and Meira against the whole world!

On New Year's Eve 1975, I'd promised to baby-sit for Arwel and Margaret so they could go out to a party. After rehearsing all day at the BBC offices in Newport Road the *Teliffant* crew had their own party, of course. I was in my element in that kind of situation, where everyone else was drinking and making merry. I could relax and socialise, and drink freely without feeling any guilt. When I left I was already late for my babysitting. That 'one last drink' had kept me at the bar like a magnet. I was drunk and legless but I still got into the car and began to make my way towards Llantrisant. It was no surprise that I failed to negotiate the turn to Creigiau and drove straight into a lamp-post. When I regained consciousness I was lying in bed at St. David's Hospital, Cardiff, with my head all bandaged up – it had gone through the windscreen – and the police were waiting to give me a breathalyser. Arwel was there, too, and I couldn't understand why he had tears in his eyes. Was it because he'd had to miss the party? The notion that someone could cry out of love for me was absurd. How could anyone love me to that extent?

Alcoholism has been described as 'the inability to feel love'. I can identify with that. Emotionally, I kept everyone at arm's length – even Meira, if I was to be perfectly honest. I used to ridicule Meira when she told me that she loved me. "Oh! Come off it!" I used to tell her. "Don't tell me your lies. How can you say you love me when I don't even love myself!" I often look back and wonder whether things would have been different had I not felt such a deep sense of rejection and being un-loved – unfounded as those feelings may have been.

Meanwhile, back home in North Wales, Meira was naturally very distressed when she heard of the accident. She was beginning to get accustomed to shocks – one crisis after another seems to be the typical pattern of an alcoholic's life – but she was really shaken by this news. Three times over the limit! A ban was inevitable. But before that there would be court proceedings and all the publicity in all the newspapers about the minister's son being fined for drink driving – and he in the business of making children's programmes! How terrible! Shameful! My imagination was running riot. In the end, however, it all passed by quietly – the one-year ban never made the headlines – and I was able to pretend, especially in North Wales, that nothing had happened.

At the beginning of 1976, we learned that Meira was expecting a baby. At the time, her father, Aneirin Owens, was dying of cancer and I was worried that she might lose the baby because of the stress. We'd been trying to have a family for ages but to no avail and we had decided to go for an adoption. The forms duly arrived but, because of my father-in-law's poor health, they were put to one side and we forgot about them. It's strange how some wishes come true when you stop striving for them! Meira conceived when we weren't even thinking of it, but when the news came I was absolutely delighted. And that was the only time since my childhood that I thanked anyone but Wynford for any blessing in my life – I thanked God.

I was going to be a dad – a sobering realisation – and, as Meira had hoped when she first suggested starting a family, I made an effort to behave sensibly. We'd need more space when the baby arrived – I was extremely busy writing scripts for *Teliffant* at the time – so I decided to build a garage and an office at the side of the house. One day a lorry arrived with a load of chippings and I had to move the car from the drive – Meira was too heavily pregnant by then – and who should pass by at that very moment but the local bobby who lived two doors away!

Unfortunately for me, the bobby had also seen me driving Meira's car around the block a week earlier – a silly act, really, for someone who had been banned from driving, but I wanted to try and hoodwink the local residents! Anyway, the outcome was an appearance at Caernarfon Magistrates Court, a hefty fine and a further one-year ban to coincide with the first. And oh yes, this time it was splashed all over the newspapers and was mentioned even on the radio and television news!

If 'inability to feel love' is a symptom of alcoholism, then I must have been perfectly sober when Bethan was born into this world on the 12th of October 1976. For I knew then what love was. I would have given my life for that perfect little bundle with a mop of black hair. And yet, whether I'd be willing to save my own life for the sake of that child, as Meira was hoping, was a different matter.

Not long afterwards, it was discovered that Mam had bowel cancer. I wasn't surprised, really, because I knew she'd been misusing laxatives and other strong tablets since she was a young girl. They were bound to have an effect on her body. And yet, when she died a few months later at the age of sixty-three, I wasn't prepared for the shock. Sixty-three! And Dad had died at the age of sixty-two. What kind of God could allow that to happen? And to two people who had served their community so well in His name for so many years? And why cruel cancer both times? It was hard to accept.

After her operation at Bangor Hospital, the family decided that Mam should spend a period of three months with each of the children, Rowenna, Arwel and me, to help her recuperate. By then, Meira was pregnant again and Mam said she was looking forward to seeing her next grandchild. Being a very determined person, she seemed to will herself to live until the baby was born. Rwth was born on the 4th of December 1977, and on the first of June the following year, Mam gave up the fight and died. Her death was a relief for the whole family because it had been a slow, cruel death. But what nagged at my conscience was the feeling that I was relieved for a different reason – my mother's illness had come between me and my first love, alcohol, and now that barrier had been removed. I didn't shed a tear at her funeral. I was in a trance, too far removed from reality to feel anything. I was certainly not in any state to appreciate the love my mother had given me throughout the years.

When Bethan was born, Meira had hoped I'd give up drinking. But that didn't happen. When Rwth came along she had high hopes again, but they were dashed a second time. I did give up drinking, actually, for a period of about two years, in an effort to stop Meira's nagging. But I substituted alcohol with other drugs – sleeping tablets, sedatives, and antidepressants. I was constantly high as a kite and I can't remember a single day of that period.

The year my mother died, 1978, was the year of my

thirtieth birthday. I had always been convinced that I'd be dead by then – dead and famous! I'd convinced Meira, too, so on my birthday she kept me in all day in case something happened to me! I'd survived so far, living with my terrible feeling of guilt and shame, only because I thought I'd die a young man, like Dylan Thomas, and that after death, as in his case, all would be forgiven. I considered myself to be a genius, and that's why I had to drink – to try to come to terms with this incredible gift I had, just like Dylan Thomas. They call it 'the tortured genius syndrome', and I suffered badly from it, as many alcoholics do.

Anyway, the day after my thirtieth birthday I was still alive! I hadn't contemplated life after thirty, really, and now all I could foresee was more of the same – the same pain, the same misery, and the same hell. I would have killed myself before then had I not been so afraid of dying. That was ironic – being afraid to die and yet causing my own slow death with alcohol! I had hoped that a car crash or a heart attack would have ended it all suddenly before my thirtieth birthday. But it hadn't happened and here I was, more afraid of the future than ever. That night I drank myself into a stupor, comforting myself that I knew of one escape route if things became unbearable. On the main road on the outskirts of Penrhyndeudraeth I'd noticed a pretty solid stone wall; a crash there could end my misery at any time.

1978 1984

FROM TELIFFANT TO HEROIN

My past was at last
catching up with me. The
time had come for me to
face the consequences
of my behaviour...

As far as *Teliffant* was concerned, this was the beginning of a turbulent period. Within the BBC in Cardiff, I was told, there had always been an argument as to which Department *Teliffant* belonged – the Children's Department or the Light Entertainment Department. Now that the programme had become very popular, there was more at stake and the debate became rather heated. In an extraordinary move to settle the matter once and for all, the Head of Programmes, Geraint Stanley Jones, decided to scrap the programme altogether! It was unbelievable!

Mici Plwm and I decided immediately to produce the programme independently. The characters in the show had taken a great deal of imagination and ingenuity to create and they had gained cult status and a huge following. Mici and I were proud of them and we were determined to keep them alive! The first idea we had was to organise a touring pantomime, but when the BBC heard of this they tried to put the kybosh on it, claiming the copyright on the characters belonged to the Corporation. Fortunately for us, our literary agent in London was able to prove otherwise and the future seemed a little brighter again.

Our first success came when Dafydd Meirion, director of the publishing company Cyhoeddiadau Mei, agreed to use the characters in the newly launched children's comic *Sboncyn*. Then we approached the director of the Wales Theatre Company with a view to creating a pantomime based on the *Teliffant* characters. With all the publicity surrounding the BBC's handling of the programme there would be no difficulty in attracting good audiences. Wilbert Lloyd Roberts was very receptive to the idea and he commissioned a pantomime script. Mici and I had great fun writing the script but when we met Wilbert again to discuss the next step, something very strange happened – he denied having ever commissioned the script. We had a contract, and it was there in black and white in front of us, but he maintained it was a commission for an outline plan only. We engaged The Writers' Guild to defend our case but Wilbert refused to budge from that new interpretation – and we didn't get paid!

We had better luck with Bwrdd Ffilmiau Cymraeg (Welsh Film Board). They commissioned us to make three short films to tour Wales. The tour itself proved to be a resounding success but, more importantly, it kept the characters alive until the coming of S4C, the Welsh-language television channel, which would provide huge job opportunities when launched in a few years' time (1982). Also, we were introduced to an excellent cameraman, Graham Edgar, with whom we would work closely for the next ten years.

The next step was to set up an independent television programme production company called Burum (Yeast) – with the aim of taking advantage of the growing market potential. (Several similar companies were set up in anticipation of the emergence of S4C.) This was a venture by Dafydd Meirion, the publisher, and myself. It seemed an ideal partnership – Dafydd a successful businessman, and me with my creative background. It did cross my mind to invite Mici Plwm to join us but in the end I decided not to. We had worked well together in creating *Teliffant* but the partnership had become increasingly strained. The problem was he knew I was an out-of-control alcoholic, and he didn't really know how to cope with the situation. He tried to get me to conform and toe the line; he tried to control my behaviour. He meant well but, to the alcoholic, anyone who tries to control their behaviour is in danger of becoming their number one enemy. In the Syr Wynff and Plwmsan partnership, the main characters in *Teliffant*, I realised that he was an essential part of the duo, and that would have to continue – but I didn't have to depend on him in any other aspect of my life. When I was in his company I felt as if I was walking on eggshells; that's the reason I didn't want him as a partner in the new company. The decision was made, basically, by my illness.

The new company's hopes were soon realised – we were commissioned by S4C to produce a series of programmes featuring Syr Wynff and Plwmsan. And when the new channel was launched on the 1st of November 1982, on the very first Friday evening, the first episode of *Anturiaethau Syr Wynff a Plwmsan* (The Adventures of Syr Wynff and Plwmsan) was broadcast. It quickly became one of the nation's favourite programmes.

We had great fun filming the series and the work even took us to locations abroad. We went to California on one occasion and did some filming with a German production team in the Universal Studios in Hollywood. The Germans loved the two mad characters and quickly realised the potential to translate the programmes into other languages. There was a huge market in Germany alone. So, in order to discuss the possibilities, the directors of the German team invited us to dinner at an expensive Chinese restaurant in Hollywood. All that was required of Mici and me was to keep our mouths shut and let our work on the small screen do the talking! Unfortunately, that was too much to ask of me.

Because alcoholics feel so inferior, they often try to portray a larger than life image of themselves, and as a result they can appear to be conceited and pompous. And that's what happened to me that night. As the tales of my brilliant achievements reached new pinnacles with every drink, and as the copyright fees I would demand reached Monopoly proportions, I saw the Germans' jaws drop with dismay. That night, in a drunken state, it shames me to recall, I blew a wonderful and very real opportunity to market the Syr Wynff and Plwmsan duo worldwide. And that was that! 'There is a tide in the affairs of men ...!'

Having failed to conquer the world in America and Germany, I set about conquering Wales. With my colleagues Dafydd Meirion and Graham Edgar, the cameraman, I set up a new lighting and resources company to service the film and television industry in Wales. We called the company MWG (Meirion, Wynford, Graham). (The word 'mwg' has two meanings in Welsh – 'smoke' and 'mug' – so you can take your pick!) Setting up this company was a knee-jerk reaction to a snub from Huw Jones, the popular singer who was now head of a television production company called Teledu'r Tir Glas (Green Land or Virgin Land Television) and who was in the process of setting up a new outside broadcasting consortium called Barcud (Kite) in Caernarfon. A meeting of potential members of the consortium was organised in Caernarfon and Mei and I had intended being there to represent Burum. On the day of the meeting, however, Mei received a telephone call from Huw Jones forbidding me from attending. He didn't want me to have any part in the new consortium. In retrospect I can appreciate his standpoint – the risk of having a drinking alcoholic as a partner in a high-stakes company was simply too great – but at the time my false pride was seriously dented. Huw Jones shot to the top of the long list of people I resented.

The next commission from S4C was a comedy series called *Bysus Bach y Wlad* (Little Country Busses). I managed to give up drinking whilst directing the actual filming and that part of the work was completed on schedule and within budget. The only method I used to distract my mind from my terrible stomach pain was to smoke the strongest cigarettes I could find. In the ensuing end-of-shoot party, however, I started drinking again and from then on the production went pear shaped. The editing work dragged on and on and I just couldn't concentrate on the task in hand. I spent most of the time in my own fantasy world. Needless to say, our production company, Burum, began to encounter difficulties. After all, how could we expect more commissioned work from S4C when one of the two partners in the company was *non compos mentis* every hour of the day?

I moved on to direct a light-hearted television chat show called *Ond O Ddifri, Madam Sera!* (But Seriously, Madame Sera!), hoping that no one at S4C Headquarters in Cardiff had twigged that I was by now out of control. Madam Sera (real name Maggie Glen) and I got on well together – both of us were too fond of the drink! But I marvelled at her ability to control her drinking and maintain some semblance of order (if not normality) in her life. She was already a well-known astrologist, having featured regularly on Hywel Gwynfryn's morning radio programme, and I admired her as a natural performer, who had an incredibly electric personality. She was the perfect subject for a light entertainment television programme. Unfortunately, my programme was sabotaged, it seemed to me, by someone in the BBC. Each time we recorded a programme, with invited guests, those very guests would often feature soon afterwards (and before our programme was broadcast) in a similar radio programme. The impression given was that we were copying their ideas, not the other way around. It seemed pretty obvious that someone (and I have my suspicions) was taking unfair advantage of our research work and claiming two payments. I couldn't prove anything, of course, but that didn't prevent me from getting really worked up about yet another example of people playing dirty tricks to undermine my credibility, my career and me as a person. There was, undoubtedly in my view, a general vendetta against me!

Various items for the *Madam Sera* show were filmed in Amsterdam and at the Felin-fach Theatre near Aberaeron in Ceredigion. During this period, we had several 'misfortunes'. On a trip to Amsterdam, the Dan Air plane was grounded and the return flight was delayed for a whole day. Our equipment was impounded at the airport so, in order to take advantage of our unexpected extra time, I decided to hire some camera equipment locally. Unfortunately, my passport was stolen from the hotel and this caused no end of problems when I tried to transfer money from my bank in Caernarfon to pay for the hired equipment. I was under considerable stress and I suddenly felt a sharp pain across my chest. 'This is it!' I thought, 'A heart attack!' My flight back to London was not helped by the loss of my passport. I was in the middle of explaining my predicament to one of the Customs officers when one of them chirped in with the words: "With an accent like that, mate, you must belong here. Get in!"

Back in Cardiff, my doctor assured me that the pain in my chest was due to stress, not a heart attack, and advised me to drink less and rest. It was impossible for me to do either! First of all, I was by now physically dependent on alcohol and, as for the 'rest', well, there were ten *Madam Sera* programmes which had to be filmed at the Felin-fach Theatre. When I got to Felin-fach I was in a terrible state. I kept tripping over the cables and the equipment and falling flat on my back in front of the audience. I was plainly drunk and incapable of performing my work. More than that, I was becoming the subject of gossip and bringing disgrace upon the new Welsh channel – at a time it needed all the support it could get.

When I returned home to Bontnewydd I had a visit from Emlyn Davies, S4C's lone programme commissioner at the time. My conduct at Felin-fach had been reported to him and he'd also received several other complaints about me, including one from a member of the film crew in Amsterdam. I wasn't surprised, really. My past was at last catching up with me. The time had come for me to face the consequences of my behaviour – something I hadn't done since I was a child. In a nutshell, the message was that due to my unacceptable behaviour, there would be no further commissioned work from S4C. It meant that I was facing a very bleak future. Burum, the television company, would have to be wound up, and quite soon both Mei and I would have to pull out of MWG, the lighting company. Worst of all, it meant the demise of the popular *Syr Wynff a Plwmsan* programmes and all the plans that had been laid for their future. All of a sudden, Emlyn Davies had jumped to the top of my hate list, well ahead of Huw Jones, Geraint Stanley Jones and even Pritch Bach, my former headmaster whose cutting comments still hurt!

After that visit from Emlyn Davies, life fell into a monotonous pattern – no work, no hope, only more drinking and more debts. Strangely, I had no feelings of sympathy for all the people who had lost their jobs because of me – people like Dafydd Meirion, Mici Plwm, Graham Edgar and a host of others employed by the company. But they were true friends to me; not one of them ever reproached me for my drinking, not once. Perhaps they understood my illness better than I did and accepted that I could do nothing about it. Or perhaps they were just kind people. Had I known that, and realised I could attract good people to me as well as the undesirable, I might have seen a glimmer of hope. But I didn't, and I descended into deep melancholia, immersed in self-pity.

That was hell. And in the midst of all this hopelessness was a small family struggling to grow up – Bethan and Rwth, with Meira trying to protect them from the worst effects of my illness. But it was impossible to protect them from every unreasonable behaviour – the negativity, and the pathetic emotional games I used to play. What I did to my two daughters can only be described as emotional rape. I took from them their right to experience natural childhood emotions – the confidence and joy of growing in a safe environment full of care and love. Instead, I expected them to understand my complex and warped emotions – when I blackmailed them by threatening to drink, to side with me against their mother and to agree with me when every reason pointed the other way. This is how an alcoholic father gets his children to join him in his own unreal world, where normality is turned upside-down, where it is natural and acceptable for the children to see him drunk at eight o' clock in the morning and being sick in the washbasin as he cleans his teeth.

But why didn't Meira leave me to spare herself and the girls from this hell? A person who really understands the illness would not ask that question. The answer is simple – it was as impossible for Meira to leave me as it was for me to stop drinking. We were locked together by the illness. I had an obsession for drinking; she was obsessed with trying to stop me! And somewhere in the middle the girls learned about life – with a father who loved alcohol more than them, and a mother who was on a crusade to ban alcohol from the house. What a dysfunctional family! Of course, there was nothing wrong with us, and woe betide anyone who suggested such a thing! That is the devilment of alcoholism – the family illness, where unhappiness and distress are conditions that are swept under the carpet and hidden from the world.

I was out of work for almost a year and I lost all confidence in my ability to perform. Apart from an occasional trip to Liverpool to see a specialist about my stomach, my life had shrunk to a daily visit to two local pubs. The rest of the time I spent gazing through the window, cursing everyone, including God, for landing me in such a hellhole.

I don't know where the inspiration came from, but I set about writing a short play. The theme was addiction – what else could it be – and the story was based on my own experience. The title I gave it was *Llef Un yn Llefain* (A Cry in the Wilderness), which was rather obviously significant.

This was the first time I'd written about the illness, and although I realised my condition had become public knowledge by then, I still didn't want my 'audience' to think the play was about me! I disguised myself as Meic, a heroin addict who was approaching premature death in a cold city flat. I'd always looked down with contempt at the wretched people addicted to heroin and other illegal drugs. My tablets were prescribed by a doctor! But I was just as addicted to Heminevrin, Prothiaden and Valium as Meic was to heroin. We were both addicts. Our minds had been contaminated to the same degree by our respective drugs and through Meic's thoughts during the last minutes of his life I was able, for the first time ever, to have a brief glimpse of my own madness.

I entered the play for the literature competition in the local *eisteddfod* at Caernarfon and the adjudicator, John Gwilym Jones, a highly respected literary figure in his own right, awarded me the first prize. Bethan won a prize too, as the most promising performer. So, after a long, long time in the wilderness I realised that there was at least a glimmer of hope that things had taken a turn for the better – if only I could find a job!

A fortnight later I had a telephone call from Graham Jones, drama producer in HTV. A new drama series, *Dinas* (City), was about to be launched on S4C and he wanted to know whether I'd be interested in playing the part of Robin Gregory, one of the main characters. I bought an extra bottle of wine to celebrate that night, praying that everything would turn out all right. Towards the end of 1984 things were looking up again, careerwise, and the dragon inside me purred like a contented old cat, for a change!

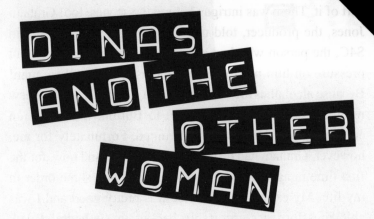

1985 1992

DINAS AND THE OTHER WOMAN

...Graham Laker spoke to me, saying
exactly the right words, in exactly the right
order, at exactly the right time...

bout the intrigues of life in the city,
great splash of publicity on the 19th
s the most expensive drama series
sh language and I was proud to be
gue behind the scenes, too! Graham
me that someone in high rank in
l commissioned the series, had put
pressure on him not to employ me as an actor. Wise man!
Because alcoholics are not dependable – and this person knew
me well, particularly in relation to Burum, the television
company that I had set up and ruined. Fortunately for me,
however, Graham had disregarded the advice and now, for the
first time in ages, I had a regular income and some order in
my life. My expenses allowance was pretty good and I was
able to afford a comfortable bed-sit in Cathedral Road,
Cardiff.

American Express soon heard of my newfound status and
I received a generous offer to own a gold card. Image is
important to the alcoholic, so an Amex Gold was certainly
something to possess. (It took some effort, though – I had to
send it back twice and ask for a new one because my signature
was unrecognisable!) This little matter is not important in
itself but it typifies the alcoholic's materialistic values, always
wanting more and more, whilst neglecting the truly important
thing in life – spiritual development.

Because of *Dinas*, I was relatively well off. I still had my
debts but at least I could pay the interest on them, and the
mortgage. I wasn't satisfied, though, and the thing that
bugged me most of all at the time was loneliness. It didn't
matter how busy my life was, or how many parties I could go

to, at the end of the day I had to return to my lonely bed-sit and face the agony of my own company. That's when the dragon would be at its worst – reminding me of my past, and the hurt I'd caused Meira and the girls. My conscience was torturing me. At thirty-seven years of age I had so many memories that I wanted to bury – or drown, rather, in alcohol and drugs of all sorts. (I had two doctors prescribing me drugs at this time, one in the north and one in the south.) But, all of a sudden, the drink and the drugs became ineffective – they were not able to change my mood any more – and I had to find something else. That 'something else' was Meira's company. If only I had her company, everything would be all right. I knew very well that she would not want to move to Cardiff, but I decided that was the only answer.

There was a time when Meira would accompany me to public functions – parties, dances and shows – but not any more. She'd been humiliated so often; me making a fool of myself and people whispering their snide remarks behind cupped hands. She now preferred to stay at home with the girls. When I started work with *Dinas* in Cardiff there was a mutual understanding that my stay there would be temporary and that I would commute on a weekly basis. After all, Meira had her own permanent job as a teacher in the north – a job that had kept us going as a family for years – and we couldn't jeopardise that, no matter how secure my contract with HTV appeared at the time.

How on earth, then, was I going to persuade Meira to change her mind? I pleaded with her and begged her, but she refused – not for her own sake, but for that of the girls. They were happily settled in their school and Meira felt it would be very upsetting and unfair to uproot them at that stage.

But when I raised the matter again a few months later she must have realised how desperate I was. She agreed straight away. Within minutes she had decided to give up her job, uproot the children from their school and their community, and move to live with me, permanently, in Cardiff – just as I wanted. She showed no hesitation whatsoever in making those difficult decisions and I must be forever grateful to her for that because, in the grand scheme of things, and despite my selfish motives at the time, our long-term recovery as a family hinged on the fact that Meira, Bethan and Rwth moved to live with me in Cardiff. When I later asked her why she'd changed her mind so suddenly, she said: "I just knew it was the right thing to do."

However, as I drove the car on that fateful journey to Cardiff, I had one of the saddest experiences of my life, with Meira at my side and the girls in the back, all breaking their hearts – and knowing I was the cause of it all. We registered the girls in the Welsh section of Creigiau Primary School – Creigiau being a most pleasant village on the outskirts of Cardiff. We knew this area because my brother, Arwel, and his family lived there. Arwel at that time was about to take up his appointment as Head of BBC Programmes in Northern Ireland – a step up from his previous post as Head of News and Current Affairs for BBC Wales. His career was at its peak – as, I must confess, was my jealousy of him.

We knew that the bed-sit in Cathedral Road was unsuitable so, for various reasons – school, Arwel's family, and the availability of a local doctor to look after the family's well-being, particularly my dependency – we set our minds on finding a house in Creigiau. At first we rented a small house – Hamster House as it was aptly named, after Bethan and Rwth's hamsters. We paid an outrageous bond of £500, and when the time came to move on, I'm afraid I had to engage in a rather devious act in order to secure the full refund! After a few months we bought a new house in Creigiau, where we still live, actually, and on the morning of the move, Tom and Hari, the two hamsters, had to be shut in the bathroom for an hour because they'd found a way of escaping from their cage. When Bethan went to fetch them she screamed in horror: "Mam! Dad! Look what Tom and Hari have done!" They'd gnawed and scratched away at the carpet leaving a great big hole just in front of the toilet. The landlord was bound to see it, and it would cost us £500! So I gathered the loose tufts and stuck them back with glue! A neat job, and the landlord didn't notice it! Today, in my current condition, I wouldn't dare to do anything dishonest because it would jeopardise my sobriety. But at the time I was ill, and I felt justified in doing a bit of cheating to retain the bond; the money could be better spent on other things – my drinks for a start! I still have pangs of guilt when I pass that house on my way to the shop!

One morning during rehearsals for *Dinas* I got into an argument with one of the directors. I don't remember what the issue was, but I remember the cause – my drunkenness. For some time I'd been drinking a quarter bottle of vodka every morning, without any visible effect. On that day, however, I'd drunk a half bottle and was pretty fractious. Who should happen to pass by at the time but Graham Jones, the producer. Without a moment's hesitation he gave me a stern warning that unless I did something about my problem at once, that very day, he would give me instant dismissal. The effect was amazing! And I've since noticed that when someone in authority, as Graham was, takes such direct and forceful action, the alcoholic tends to respond.

I immediately contacted a friend of mine, an alcoholic who had been in recovery for some time, and he helped me to stop drinking – for a while. It was short-lived, though. The motivation was simply to keep my job, not to gain sobriety. And since I hadn't been to jail, or beaten my wife, or lost my job – not yet anyway – I came to the conclusion that I wasn't really an alcoholic after all. My friend's experiences were not relevant to me. Meira was glad I'd come to that conclusion, too. The last thing she wanted was to be an alcoholic's wife!

I convinced myself that the root cause of my drink problem was my stomach pain and my loneliness – despite now having my family around me. I was willing to go on the wagon to please Graham, but if that was to be the case, I'd have to convince my doctor (the one in North Wales) to prescribe me stronger tablets. I also made one other important decision – I was going to suggest to Graham that Robin Gregory, the character I played in the drama, should himself develop a drink problem. In this way the series could deal with topical problems and real-life situations, and increase its popular appeal. Graham was impressed and, so, with this one stroke of creative genius I achieved two goals – meeting Graham's ultimatum and also securing a future for the character (and my job) in the series.

The reality of the situation, in fact, was pathetic. In one scene a little later, in a meeting room for alcoholics, there were two of us discussing our problems over a cup of tea.

There we were, pontificating on the merits of refraining from drinking alcohol whilst we slipped out to the toilet every whipstitch to swig vodka!

Wherever I went, I took my briefcase with me, containing a quarter bottle of vodka, a bottle of Night Nurse (there's more alcohol in this medicine than sense!), and some sleeping tablets, sedatives and antidepressants. Of these tablets the most important were the sleepers. Once every three months I visited my GP in North Wales and he would prescribe me three months' supply. Every single day I'd count my sleeping tablets, making sure I had at least three for each night. Once or twice a week I'd take four, as a treat! Obviously, the supply ran out well before the end of the three months. But all I had to do was pick up the phone to my doctor (I was on good terms with him), and he'd send me some more by post. Anyway, the important thing about all this was that I was able to give Graham the impression that my drinking problem was under control!

But it wasn't, really. One night, after drinking heavily, I had a flare-up with Meira and went to the bedroom in a temper with the intention of killing myself. Suicide was always an option for me although I was afraid of dying. I swallowed about twenty-five strong sleeping tablets and went to bed. I woke up in the Royal Glamorgan Hospital in Church Village (where it was located then) with Meira sitting at my bedside, a forlorn figure, and a sinister sign above my bed – 'Overdose'. Even in that situation I had managed to humiliate Meira. She told me afterwards: "I felt so silly. I couldn't tell the doctor what tablets you were on. They're always locked up in that bloody briefcase of yours. I couldn't say what tablets my own husband was on!"

The next step was to see a psychiatrist in the local mental hospital. It didn't take long for me to persuade him to prescribe me some drugs to replace my supply from North Wales, which had now dried up. That doctor had been reprimanded – almost deregistered – when it became known that he'd been supplying me by post.

It was more difficult to hoodwink Arwel. He'd been called to my bedside, along with my GP, on the morning following my failed suicide attempt and he was gravely concerned. I tried to make light of it all, saying it was just an unfortunate accident. But he would have none of it. I knew then that at last, after all these years, someone in the family had had a glimpse of what was really going on within our home. I was deeply ashamed of myself and thanked the Lord that my mother and father had been spared the truth about their Hyacinth. I implored Arwel not to tell my sister, Rowenna.

In the meantime, news came through that Ffilmiau Llifon, a newly formed film production company, was interested in making a new series of *Anturiaethau Syr Wynff a Plwmsan*. The company's director, Gareth Lloyd-Williams, clearly saw an opportunity to establish himself and the new company with material that was a guaranteed success! But I didn't mind that as long as Mici Plwm and I were dealt a fair deal. It transpired that this series of six programmes was the best of the lot, technically.

Mici Plwm and I are still great friends, which is surprising given the traumas we've been through together. The main reason for this close friendship, I believe, is that both of us had dedicated our whole lives, more or less, to these two mad characters. That may have been good for our friendship, and I have no regrets on that front, but from the professional and career point of view, I can see now that clinging to those characters for so long had stereotyped me and severely stinted my development. In retrospect, I can see how clinging to the familiar gave me a degree of security at a time when my self-esteem was at a very low ebb. It is only now, in my sobriety, that I have been able to break away from that and have the confidence to do other things.

Following the retirement of Owen Edwards as the pioneering chief of S4C, Geraint Stanley Jones was appointed to the post of Chief Executive. This news frightened me, for he was still near the top of my hate list and I was convinced that the reason he'd taken up the post was in order to destroy my career! Just a slight touch of paranoia! But here he was – the former Head of Programmes with BBC Wales, former Controller of BBC Wales and former member of the Governing Body of the BBC in London – coming back to Wales with the sole purpose of destroying me! It just goes to show how inflated my ego was at the time.

Paranoia or not, my fears were more or less justified. It was soon announced that the *Syr Wynff a Plwmsan* series was to end in 1989. Mici Plwm and I were outraged and we arranged a campaign to save the popular characters. A petition with 15,000 signatures was presented to the S4C bigwigs at the Urdd National Eisteddfod at Dyffryn Nantlle in 1990, but to no avail. We also felt betrayed by certain persons who we thought could have done more to support us, and we said some nasty things about them. But the truth of the matter was that Mici and I were two people who had come to depend too much on something (the series, in this case) and were trying to do everything within our power to make sure the dependency did not come to an end. We both felt comfortable inside the two characters we had created; it was familiar territory and we didn't want to break with it. In a way, we were imprisoned. The parallel with alcohol dependency is obvious. The reaction to any attempt at weaning can be furious, and it is based on fear – fear of the unfamiliar, fear of the future. And however much the alcoholic or the drug addict wants to end the dependency, they are shackled to the familiar and breaking away is very, very difficult.

As I mentioned before, despite having my family around me, I still suffered a feeling of loneliness. It was like being in a glass jar, aware of the people around me but with an impenetrable barrier between us. This is how I try to explain the fact that during the filming of the final series of *Syr Wynff a Plwmsan*, I had an affair with another woman. Suddenly, this other person became the most important thing in my life. She was the one who would fill the void inside me; she was the one who was going to change everything for the better! Forget Meira and the children. Forget the rest of my family and my few remaining friends. Forget the hurt that this affair would inflict on all of them. Filling the unbearable void inside me was the most important thing in the world, more important than alcohol, even, for a while. Familiar story?

Alcohol and drugs are not the only things that can enslave people. I was also addicted to food, to work, and to sex. This poor woman was swept into the mad merry-go-round of that last addiction. During that dark period she believed all my lies and became prey to my insatiable desire to boost my self-image, whatever the cost. Ironically, it is a sad fact that dependency on alcohol and other drugs over a long period of time causes impotency, and my performance in that department wasn't up to much by then! What really mattered to me, and what gave me that boost of self-belief, was the fact that here was a young woman, a mother of two children, willing to sacrifice everything just to be with me. The parallel with Meira, and the fact I already enjoyed such a privileged situation wasn't enough. Typical of my condition, I just wanted more and more.

It wasn't that I'd fallen out of love with Meira or stopped loving my two daughters – to the contrary, they meant a great deal to me. But that's not what I told my new partner. I told her that my marriage was a sham and that we'd kept together simply for the children's sake. To be fair to my new partner, I don't think she would have continued the relationship had she not truly believed that to be the case because she, too, was locked in an unhappy marriage and believed our new-found friendship to be an escape route to happiness for both of us.

This relationship put both families under tremendous pressure. To Meira, this new threat to our marriage had suddenly overtaken my alcoholism as her main worry. She put up with my drinking at home concentrating, instead, on trying to get me to realise the harm I was doing to everyone that was dear to me. I promised everything to everyone. To Meira I promised to end the affair; to my other partner I promised to continue the relationship. I knew full well that the whole affair could only end in tears, and yet I felt powerless to do anything to stop the mad merry-go-round.

I decided to leave my family. Then I went back. My sister

begged me to stay with Meira but I ignored her pleading and left once again. My new partner decided to leave her family, too, and moved from North Wales to live in Cowbridge. By way of a strange sense of 'decorum', she insisted that I should live on my own in a flat before moving in to live with her! Live on my own for a year? I couldn't live on my own for two minutes, let alone a year! She just didn't understand the nature of my problem – that I hated myself too much to bear my own company, and that the only reason for having the affair with her was to try to escape from myself!

I expect it would be difficult for any reasonable person to understand such irrational thinking. The only explanation I can offer, in retrospect, is that I sensed that my marriage was in a precarious state and the relationship with the other woman was all about avoiding the inevitable heightened sense of isolation that would follow a break-up. It was all about arranging things so that I would step without much disruption from one relationship into the other, thus by-passing the hell of being on my own. The proposition of staying in a flat, on my own, was out of the question, so back I went to Meira.

During this period, when things became unbearable, I visited the mental hospital in Whitchurch, Cardiff. The psychiatrist's diagnosis was 'emotional problems' – nothing to do with alcohol! "It's because of the affair, Wynford, and the guilt associated with causing so much hurt to your wife and children." I was placed in a secure psychiatric ward but, for some reason, I was allowed to come and go as I pleased. I spent every day getting drunk in the nearest pub!

In the midst of all this madness, S4C decided that *Dinas* should be discontinued. I was past caring – there was a greater disaster looming in my life! Anyway, I was offered work with a small theatre company, Arad Goch (Red Plough), based in Aberystwyth. Gwenlyn Parry, a well-known Welsh playwright, had recently died and, as a tribute to his memory, the company wanted to stage one of his plays on a tour of the country. The offer was gladly accepted. It would provide me with another opportunity to escape from the hell I was suffering at the time. I remember feeling envious of Gwenlyn Parry – that he'd been allowed to escape for good!

During the first week of rehearsals in Aberystwyth I drank heavily and swallowed tablets by the handful. By the end of the week I could hardly speak. My voice was husky, my stammer was at its worst, and learning my words was an impossible task.

As I travelled home on the Saturday morning, I was suddenly paralysed by fear – a feeling of trepidation, a premonition that something terrible was about to happen to me; that I was going to die. I got as far as Rhaeadr in Mid Wales but couldn't go any further. There was nothing for it but to abandon my car and hire a taxi all the way home, to Creigiau, near Cardiff (at a hefty cost that considerably swelled my debt, which was already thousands of pounds). I spent the rest of the weekend in bed. My sister and brother-in-law came to see me, inquisitive to know what was wrong with me, but it was Meira who fobbed them off with a quick "Oh. It's only a bug!" as the illness continued, with everyone afraid to confront the obvious truth – that I was an alcoholic.

The following Monday I went back to Aberystwyth to work on the play, but the drinking continued with a vengeance until, one day, I collapsed. Mrs. Ellis, landlady of the

Shangrila, the small guesthouse where I was staying, called Dr. Richard Edwards, and there's no doubt that I owe my life to those two people. He diagnosed acute liver malfunction which could prove to be life threatening. (The blood test consequently showed a liver function reading in the high eight hundreds, which is well up in the danger zone.) He ordered me to stop drinking – with immediate effect – and I promised to call in his surgery every morning on the way to rehearsals so that he could monitor my progress.

On hearing this news, Meira came to Aberystwyth to look after me. (This wasn't the first time she'd given up several days of her teaching job to help me out.) Meira and Dr. Richard Edwards, between them, were able to keep me off alcohol for the rest of the rehearsal period, and by working into the small hours every night I managed to learn the script. To everyone's relief, particularly Jeremy Turner, the director, the tour was a success. There is no doubt in my mind that my survival during this episode was due entirely to Meira and Dr. Richard.

However, uninvited and unbeknown to me, the 'other woman' came to see the play when it visited Theatr Ardudwy in Harlech. It was 'inspirational' said she, who couldn't understand a word of Welsh! And that was it! It only took that brief encounter to undo all that Meira and Dr. Richard had achieved with me in the previous weeks. She accepted that I was not going to move into a flat to live on my own for a year – and the relationship was rekindled, along with all the attached madness.

There followed a long period of heavy drinking interrupted only by long telephone calls to the partner (seven hundred pounds in one quarter) and to a few other important people who I slandered, no doubt, in my drunken state. It was a bleak time, financially, as there were no offers of work (not surprisingly) except for one small part in a Saunders Lewis play directed by Graham Laker. He was the only one who offered me anything, and I am grateful to him for that. Otherwise it was the same routine day in day out with the occasional visit to the mental hospital.

Much later, in April 1997, I took part in a Welsh-language radio programme in which I described a typical day in my life during this period. It went like this:

Well, the first task is to try and remember what happened the night before. Perhaps Meira had been hurt – she's very quiet – and the girls are aware of that. The whole atmosphere is tense and unpleasant. The girls go to school and then I get up and go to the bathroom to clean my teeth ... and the pain in my stomach makes me sick ... and I retch and retch ... and retch again and again. Then I calculate how much time I have before the girls come home from school ... half past eight ... seven hours. If I have a bottle of wine now the effect will have worn off by then!

So, I go and sit on the bathroom toilet – I have to sit on the toilet because once I start drinking the wine I have this terrible diarrhoea! And there I sit, romanticising on how wonderful life can be! It still gives me a kick, for a short while. It doesn't take long to finish the bottle, and I start counting again. 'Oh! It's only nine o'clock ... I'll have ... another bottle!'

The rest of the day is lost!

All through this period, Bethan and Rwth were living two separate lives – one outside the home, in school and with their friends, and the other when they came home from school to find the front door open, the dog roaming the estate, and their father lying on the bed, drunk and unconscious. And this is what Meira came home to, day after day. How we survived as a family, I don't know. How we held on to some friends, also, is difficult to fathom. But we did, and to those loyal few I am greatly indebted because they proved to us that not everyone was against us.

At the time, however, my own love was misplaced. I had no feelings for anyone but my new partner – and I decided to move in with her. I well remember the day I broke the news to Meira, Bethan and Rwth that I was leaving them for good. I was on my way to Bangor to take part in *The Druid's Rest* by Emlyn Williams – again thanks to Graham Laker, my one and only employer – and I thought it was an opportune moment to make the final break. It was a beautiful, sunny day outside, but in the lounge Meira was breaking her heart, with the two girls trying desperately to comfort her. "Why, Wyn? What have I done wrong?" It's strange how the victim invariably takes the blame. But in my own mind I was convinced I was doing the right thing, and that I was being totally unselfish. "It'll be for your good in the long run," I said, full of self-pity. "You deserve someone much better than me!"

"But it's you we *want*, Dad. Why can't you *understand* that?" I was shaken by the intensity of passion in Bethan's voice. And in her eyes I caught a glimpse of all the years of hurt that I'd inflicted on the family. Those words, and those eyes, were to gnaw away at my conscience for days until, in the end, I yielded completely to my illness and cried for help.

As I was about to step into my car, Arwel arrived. He saw the tears in the girls' eyes and instinctively knew what was happening. He also knew that the cause of all the trouble was my alcoholism.

"Wynford!" he said quietly. "Why can't you be brave?"

"Be brave?" I replied indignantly, feeling that what I was about to do was the bravest and most unselfish thing anyone could ever imagine.

"Be brave? What on earth do you mean, Arwel?"

"You know very well what I mean," he said, looking me straight in the eye. "Why don't you face up to this illness and do something about it?"

I just laughed in his face. "What illness?" I shrugged my shoulders with one final question: "Why doesn't anybody understand me?" And with a dramatic pause to make sure everyone got the message, I stepped into the car and drove out of their lives.

When I arrived in Bangor, I had nowhere to stay. I couldn't stay with my sister and brother-in-law in Llanfair-pwllgwyngyll – out of both fear and shame. Two members of the theatre staff were kind enough to offer me their sofa to sleep on for a night, or may be longer, I don't remember. I remember hardly anything at all of that first week of the rehearsals – except the Friday morning, when Graham Laker spoke to me, saying exactly the right words, in exactly the right order, at exactly the right time, which caused me to do something about my alcoholism.

I'd been sitting in the car, swigging my vodka, when I was called back to rehearsal. I stumbled, drunk, into the room where Graham was waiting. He held my gaze and said in a sad voice: "When are you going to do something about your drinking, Wynford?" That's all, but the timing was perfect. For at that very moment I was ready to respond. After twenty-six years of drinking, at last I was ready to do something about my problem.

I'd heard of Rhoserchan, the treatment centre for addictive illnesses near Aberystwyth. Meira had mentioned it several times, urging me to contact them. She'd also mentioned a certain Joe South who had founded the centre and who worked there as a team leader – renowned for his ability to break down the 'denial' barrier. But I'd never been in the right condition to respond – until now. I mumbled my answer to Graham: "I'm ready. I want to go to Rhoserchan." These few words were to change my life completely, and the lives of Meira, Bethan and Rwth.

Things moved very quickly after that, as if the whole world was willing me on. Someone contacted Rhoserchan and, yes, they could take me in that afternoon. I had to be there by four o'clock. Rhys Richards, one of the actors, very kindly looked after the travel arrangements. Then I contacted Meira, for the first time in almost a week, to tell her what was happening. I asked her not to tell anyone, particularly the 'other woman'. After that phone-call I experienced a strange feeling of relief, somehow, although nothing had been resolved yet.

I was also relieved when Graham told me not to worry about my part in the play, that he would explain the situation to the cast and ask them to keep it confidential. That was important to me. What would people say? It was a bonus, too, that I wouldn't have to risk any critical reviews! All in all it seemed that, at last, things were going my way.

I travelled to Rhoserchan by taxi and, having stopped in every off-licence on the way, I arrived late ... and drunk. I banged on the door and a lady, one of the counsellors, came to open up. She looked at me as if in shock and said:

"You're drunk!"

"Yesssss. So what?" I replied, leaning shakily against the doorframe.

"Well, you're not coming in here in that state!" she said, shutting the door in my face.

I was stunned! Here was a centre for treating alcoholics – and I was being turned away because I'd been drinking! "Bitch! What are alcoholics supposed to do except drink?" I shouted. But there was no reply.

Today, I realise how indebted I am to that counsellor for rejecting me. The time wasn't right – I still had two days' drinking in me – and timing is everything. A few hours one way or the other can mean life or death to the alcoholic. I dread to think what might have happened had I been allowed in on that Friday afternoon!

The Shangrila in Aber was my only hope. When Mrs. Ellis came to the door she did recognise me, and would gladly have taken me in had she not been fully booked. But she arranged for me to stay in a terraced house with her friends, Ceredig and Bet – two lovely people who showed me compassion and love and to whom I shall be forever grateful. Bet, later, was to be the one to help me through my greatest hour of need.

The next day I contacted Dr. Meredydd Evans. I was

afraid of being on my own and, for some reason, Merêd was the name that came to mind; he had a certain charisma which drew me to him. We spent the whole day together and he was a great comfort to me. I couldn't stop drinking, and he didn't try to deter me from doing so. What he did, however, was give me a book called *Y Cynganeddion Cymreig* (a book about verse in strict metre), and said I could keep it as a gift – as long as I gave up drinking. I still have the book! After Merêd left, I felt I needed to speak to Meira again – strange behaviour for one who had just told his wife he was leaving her for good! The 'other woman' had been asking about me, wondering where I was. Meira had told her she didn't know where I was, adding: "You do realise, don't you, that he's a very sick man!" She just hung up, apparently.

My mother's youngest brother, Uncle Ed, lived in Aberystwyth. He'd always been friendly towards me ... and I knew he had a wine cabinet! So that would be a good place to visit on the Sunday morning. A sudden phone-call from 'Betty's youngest', already drunk at eleven o' clock, fixed that and an invitation to lunch. Any semblance of self-respect on my part soon evaporated and by the end of the afternoon his wine cabinet was empty. Uncle Ed must have been taken aback with my behaviour; to have someone he hadn't seen for some time pleading for a drink in the same breath as saying 'hello' was odd enough, but then to have him crying and talking of committing suicide interspersed with bouts of diarrhoea and being sick, bordered on the surreal, if not the absurd!

The defining moment in my life happened that Sunday evening, the 20th of July 1992, as I was standing outside an off-licence in the town, with a newly opened bottle of vodka in my hand. Suddenly, I had a glimpse of my real self. For that moment, and I have no idea how long it lasted, the 'denial' I had suffered all those years suddenly lifted like a mist and I saw myself for what I really was – a drunken alcoholic. The blame game disappeared with the mist. No longer did I blame my long-dead parents for what had happened to me; no longer did I blame my wife or my children, or my brother and sister, or our friends. More importantly, I realised I couldn't blame myself, either. I didn't have a choice in this matter. At last I accepted where the blame lay – in my relationship with alcohol! It was alcohol that was making all the important decisions in my life – alcohol and all the tablets I was taking, as well as all the other addictions. I was completely under their control and there was nothing I could do about it.

That fateful moment on the 20th of July 1992 was like the breaking of a new dawn. I heard a voice screaming in my head as if awakening me from a bad dream: "It's all over, Wynford! Everything is going to be alright!" And it wasn't the dragon's voice – nothing like it – for it didn't come from the same place. The dragon's voice used to come from somewhere deep down in my solar plexus; this voice came from the region of my heart. It kept ringing in my head: "It's all over! It's going to be alright. It's going to be alright."

Then, as the darkness retreated, I began to feel a strong desire to recover – to make the most of this new day in my life – and I was willing to do anything, yes anything, to escape from the clutches of my illness. I was ready to yield to a higher power – to any power – to give me the strength I needed to recover. A warm and comforting feeling of 'acceptance' began to glow inside me. No more did I hate myself for what I was or for what I had done – I accepted it all as an essential process leading up to this glorious moment. All of a sudden everything seemed perfect as it was; I didn't want any more from life than this – to accept who I was, what I was, and to start building a new life.

Slowly, I pulled myself together and made my way back to Ceredig and Pat's terraced house where I took a handful of antidepressant tablets. (I hadn't yielded completely yet!) I lay on the bed and went into a deep sleep and the strangest of dreams. In 1998 I wrote a play called *Gwin Coch a Fodca* (Red Wine and Vodka) for Theatre Powys. In it I described what I had seen in my dream that night in 1992:

> I was drinking pure water from the fountain of life and, for the first time ever, my soul was satisfied. My parents were there. So, too, were some of the dear people I'd known as a child and who had loved me unconditionally. It dawned on me that death did not exist – it was nothing but an illusion and, with that, all fear of death vanished. I became aware that my life had a purpose – that I should use it to further God's work in the world. I also realised, quite clearly, that before I could achieve anything, I had a long journey of recovery ahead of me, both physically and mentally – and that I needed help!

When I came round on Monday morning I couldn't move. I was completely paralysed. I lay there, staring at the ceiling, overwhelmed with fear that I'd had a stroke. Feelings of guilt flooded my mind. Was this God's punishment for all my sins? I'd always been taught that He was the God of revenge and retribution – God is watching! God never sleeps! Was this it?

After a while, I was able to move my lips and I managed to squeak the words, "Heeelp! ... Heeelp!". It seemed like an eternity before Bet came in. She gazed at me in a state of shock. Then, gradually, she helped me to my feet and I recall the amount of effort and concentration it required to achieve just that – and total dependence on Bet. Suddenly I began to shake uncontrollably from the DTs (*delirium tremens*). Bet held my hands tightly in hers and there we were, both of us, shaking like the proverbial jelly in the middle of the bedroom.

Then I muttered words that came from the depths of my soul: "Oh God! Please help me, God!" And with that, I yielded absolutely and accepted the fact that I was an alcoholic.

The long journey had begun!

The effects of that day are still with me. The Voice, like a friend, a soul mate, speaks to me every single day and is a source of encouragement and strength. The desire to recover, and the willingness to continue the process, is what kicks me out of bed in the morning, gets me reading *The Plain Man's Book of Prayer* by William Barclay and other books about recovery, which are essential reading to me. It gives me the courage to be myself, to share my experiences with others and help them, if I can, along the journey. It also makes me seek spiritual enrichment through daily meditation. The more I obey the Voice, the better my life becomes, somehow. I ask for nothing, I expect nothing... and I accept everything that comes my way.

THE DEVIL IN A NURSE'S UNIFORM

The lingering strands of 'denial'
which had fettered me so
stubbornly were finally broken and I
could now see the addiction for
what it really was – an illness.

I didn't properly understand the situation at the time, but the purpose of my visit to Rhoserchan, the recovery centre, on the Friday afternoon was for me to be assessed. (These assessments are essential in order to differentiate between alcoholism and alcohol abuse, two conditions that can be treated, and other, psychotic illnesses for which the addiction recovery programme is inappropriate.) These assessments cannot be undertaken if the patient is under the influence of alcohol, and that's the reason why I was turned away. However, the process was to resume on the following Monday and, if I were deemed suitable for treatment, I would be placed on the waiting list. But Dr. Huw Edwards, a consultant psychiatrist, decided that I needed a detoxification period before even being assessed by Rhoserchan – to be weaned not only from alcohol but also from Valium, because a sudden termination of the use of these substances can cause heart failure, apparently. He arranged for me to go to the mental hospital in North Road, Aberystwyth.

After that heart-felt cry for help when I was with Bet, I yielded completely. I had no fight left in me, no resistance at all, and they could do what they liked with me. In the midst of all the turmoil that morning, I telephoned Meira – again. I can't explain why but, suddenly, in this new crisis, I felt a deep need to be in contact with her. So when she asked if I'd like her to come and see me in Aber, my answer was a sincere and emphatic "Yes. Please!"

Lying in my bed in the ward that afternoon I heard footsteps in the corridor – quick and positive, with an air of determination. We embraced each other. I was so, so glad to see her! Meira had seen me in this kind of situation many times before, and when the chips were down her support, and her love, had always been there for me. I'd say "Sorry!", a word that came to me so easily, and the crisis would be over. I was so relieved when she said that despite the 'parting' a week earlier, she still wanted to 'hold on' to me – but this time things had to change. I sensed a certain assertiveness in her – and in that word 'but' there emerged a certain 'distance' between us, which I knew could only be bridged on that one condition – that things changed! Perhaps she'd been hurt just once too often! Perhaps she'd decided that she and the girls had had enough.

This was my first experience of what is known as 'emotional detachment', and I had an uneasy feeling that saying "Sorry!" would not be enough this time round. Suddenly, for the first time ever, I felt the onus was on me to take responsibility for the situation. "Sorry!" yes, but the word had to be turned into action – long-term action – if I wanted to save our marriage and all that it meant to so many people. This time, I'd have to stay sober.

I was given injections of vitamin B12 (complex) and very soon I felt reinvigorated. Due to the lack of a sensible and balanced diet, alcoholics are often deficient in this important vitamin, which can affect the nervous system, appetite and sleep. All of a sudden I began to sleep better; I began to enjoy my food; the stomach cramps became less severe, and I started doing some physical exercise, walking miles every day, up and down the prom, morning and afternoon. Just as important, I was given something definite to look forward to. In a week's time, the National Eisteddfod was coming to Aberystwyth and, as Bethan was taking part in the competition, Meira promised to bring the girls to see me. During this period, I was put on a course of Librium, a drug that, in about ten days, would help wean me off alcohol, Valium and the other drugs I'd been taking. My body should be fairly cleansed by then – but the mind was a different matter!

Although the urge to drink had gone, the alcoholic mind was still with me, critical and judgemental as ever. I was resentful towards everyone and everything, but I still justified my own behaviour. Now that my secret (as I thought) was out, how would people react? I imagined no one would want anything to do with me; no one would want to employ me; I'd become a bankrupt; I'd lose the house... Juggling with all these thoughts was rather depressing! As it turned out, however, what happened was the direct opposite. Instead of disparagement and criticism, I received goodwill and support from everyone. People were so glad that at last I was actually doing something about my alcoholism – with emphasis on the word 'doing'. I realised, and I accepted, that promises without action count for nothing.

Rhoserchan, then, was my only option. I had finally accepted that I could never conquer this illness on my own – it was too strong for me. If I was to succeed I'd need the right conditions and the right tools – I'd need advice and support on a daily basis – and Rhoserchan was the only place that could provide that. The only snag was that a three-month course would cost over four thousand pounds – and I just couldn't afford it. I already had a bank overdraft of twelve thousand pounds!

As I lay in bed one night, pondering, I was visited by the

Devil himself. He came in the guise of the attractive young nurse who was looking after me. When I explained that I couldn't sleep because I was apprehensive about going to Rhoserchan and worried about the family and what might become of us, she put her arm around me and said, in a tender voice: "You're not an alcoholic, Wynford. You just want to punish yourself for hurting your family, for the affair with the other woman and for damaging your children. That's why you want to go to Rhoserchan, Wynford – to punish yourself. 'Cos it's tough there, you know. You're not going to like it."

I looked at her in astonishment. How dare she say such a thing – when I knew full well that I was an alcoholic. How dare she jeopardise my whole future, knowing that the least excuse is enough for the alcoholic to start drinking again! My blood went cold as I sensed that I was in the presence of an evil spirit! Because I accepted I was an alcoholic – and a chronic one at that – and because I accepted I had to take responsibility to do something about it, thank God, I had the strength to tell her to go away and leave me alone. I was aware that this strength had come, not from within me, but from a 'higher power', which I've mentioned before. I said 'thank God' just then, as people often do, without really thinking about the words! Since then I've become quite sure of where I stand on that score, but others are entitled to their own views. What is not in question is that alcoholics of my type will seldom succeed in their struggle to recover without the help of some 'higher power', whatever form it may take. Dave Allen, the comedian, used to end his shows with the words: "... and may *your* God go with you." There's a lot of meaning in that!

The National Eisteddfod came and with it came the family, as promised. Although I was still a patient in the psychiatric ward, I was allowed to spend a lot of time with Meira and the girls and their friends. At first I was a bit apprehensive about meeting Bethan and Rwth's friends, who were staying with them in the caravan, but not once did I feel uncomfortable in their company. This was the closest we'd ever come to being a normal family. It was a bit odd that Dad had to say 'so-long' and go back to a mental hospital at the end of every day, but that didn't spoil the pleasure of being with them.

Earlier that week I'd been assessed by the Rhoserchan staff and accepted for treatment, with the admission date fixed for the 10th of August – just after the Eisteddfod. Dr. Huw Edwards, my consultant psychiatrist, decided that I should stay in the ward until then. He saw grave dangers in my going back to Cardiff even for a few days. The only unresolved issue was the small matter of a fee of four thousand pounds! Meira suggested that I should ask Arwel and Rowenna for a loan, but I was rather reluctant. In the end, however, I swallowed my pride and plucked up the courage to ask. Meira was quite right – they were only too pleased to help me!

I was taken to Rhoserchan by Meira, Bethan and Rwth before they returned to Cardiff. There were lots of tears. I hated tears, especially Meira's. I'd seen too many of them over the years, I suppose. "See what you've done to your family?" That was my first greeting at the centre before being led to my bedroom to have my bags searched. All newcomers had their bags searched in case alcohol or other drugs were being smuggled in.

The centre could take twelve patients at a time. The building was made up of two single storey wooden huts linked by two short corridors with an entrance and a small flower garden to the front and a huge vegetable garden to the rear, where a horse and some cats were kept. It was self-sufficient in vegetables and fruit, and gardening was part of the treatment. In fact, the recovery programme treated the whole person – body, mind and spirit – and was based on instilling hope, order and discipline into the alcoholics' lives and teaching them to accept responsibility. The idea came from America – the 'Minnesota Model' – a treatment programme developed by Hazelden in Minnesota in 1949 and which is now used world-wide to treat addiction.* The first and most vital step in the process was to break down the patients' 'denial', and this was achieved through relentless questioning, and challenging them to confront the consequences and the damage caused by their drinking in the past, until they yielded and reached a state of 'acceptance'. Only then, when they were ready to conform and become teachable, could the actual recovery begin. It was a tough regime, but effective.

The process certainly worked for me. In fact, I was such a stubborn customer, I don't think any other method would have worked with me. But not everybody agreed. Some patients found the programme too confrontational, and left. We must accept that the treatment that works for one alcoholic may not be suitable for another – and there are alternative models and interventions. However, I suspect that many of

*This was an adaptation of the 12 Step Alcoholics Anonymous recovery programme adopted by the US Government to treat soldiers who had become addicted to alcohol and other drugs while on duty in Vietnam. Hundreds of these centres were set up throughout the country and they proved to be very successful.

those who left Rhoserchan did so because their illness was stronger than their desire to recover; that they resisted yielding because they wanted to drink again. And this was such a tragedy, because by abandoning the help that was being offered, I knew they were going to kill themselves with alcohol or some other drug. It was inevitable. I'd witnessed it so often over the years – and it's one of the worst ways of dying.

For the first six weeks the main focus of attention was the harm I had done to myself and others. Day in day out I'd write down at least three examples of how my drinking had affected me and other people, and the damage I had caused. If you do that for three weeks it becomes tedious. Do it for six weeks and it becomes really irksome. Evidence of the consequences of your drinking is all around you in black and white. It's impossible to avoid the fact that you are an alcoholic; in the end you have to accept it. The Devil in a nurse's uniform at the hospital was right about one thing – it was tough at Rhoserchan! But it wasn't the persistent challenging that made it tough. Rather, it was the fact that you were encouraged to examine your own situation – to have a really close look at yourself, the bad and the ugly, without the help of alcohol or any other drug to ease the pain. Discovering the truth about myself was, indeed, a painful process. But it had its blessings, too, because I also discovered some elements of good in me – providing me with a foundation on which I could begin to rebuild my life.

There were regular group therapy sessions at which the patients had to share their experiences, including their hopes for the future. My problem with this was that I didn't have any hope to share with anyone – my world was completely dark and hopeless – and as soon as I'd dealt with one problem, another would raise its ugly head.

One day a letter arrived from 'the other woman' – somehow she'd discovered my whereabouts – and, as you'd expect, it was a pretty angry letter. After all, I had destroyed that young woman's life. She now lived on the outskirts of Cardiff, her marriage broken, and not knowing what had happened to the person who caused that breakdown in the first place. Guilt and compassion came to me in equal shares and I drafted a reply to try to explain things – my illness and my changed circumstances. After discussing my reply with the group, however, I had to rewrite it completely. The fundamental question was: "Wynford! Do you want the affair to continue?"

The answer was "No!", of course. By then I could see the affair for what it really was – an escape route if things got too difficult at home. It was a means of avoiding a situation where I'd be on my own, alone, whilst at the same time enabling me to continue my drinking habit uninterrupted. It was as simple as that!

I was advised to end the relationship there and then, without leaving any doors ajar for the affair to start up again at a later date. My reply would have to be short, cruel – and final. In the group discussion I was told in no uncertain terms that if I was serious about recovering, then that had to be my number one priority. No compromise was possible. And I had no option.

By the end of the first week I thought I'd convinced everyone what an honest and sincere person I was. But not

Joe, my personal counsellor! "I don't know how you do it, Wynford – but you're nothing of the sort!" he told me. "You're devious and dishonest!" He'd seen through me from the beginning; he was familiar with the tactics I used to win people over – the winking, the flattery, the blarney, all the usual smooth charm – and he wasn't taken in by any of it. "From now on," he said, "you have to be ruthlessly honest – with yourself and with everybody else." It was a tall order, but I gradually got there and eventually I was able to discuss my feelings quite openly with the group.

As part of the process, a questionnaire was sent to Meira and the girls, and I had to fill one in too. Listening to the girls' answers being read out to the group was a painful experience. That was the first time Meira, Bethan and Rwth had been perfectly honest and open about their feelings towards me when I was drinking – and it hurt. That's when I realised the full extent of the damage I'd caused.

When I read out my own response to the questionnaire, everyone was surprised at the tender feelings I had for others, especially my parents. I described them as the perfect parents, especially Mam, whom I lavished with praise as the best mother anyone could ever have had.

After the session Joe called me into his room for a chat. I was about to discover how harsh the language of recovery has to be – no place for sentiment, no room for any woolly interpretation, no escape from the bare truth! It can be an excruciatingly painful experience.

"You describe your mother as the 'the perfect mother', Wynford!"

"Yes," I replied. "My mother meant everything to me,

Joe. She was perfect in every way. A spectacular woman!"

"I think not!" he said, and my stomach tightened, because I sensed what was coming. "Your mother suffered from an illness, Wynford. She was hopelessly addicted to barbiturates. She was obsessive, compulsive, and also bulimic, Wynford – when the word hadn't even been invented."

These were words I didn't want to hear. They brought back unpleasant memories. But I knew they were true.

"How d'you know all this, Joe?" I asked.

"It was all in your questionnaire! I know all the signs, Wynford – the addictive process, the addictive behaviour. It was all there."

Damn it! I thought. I've betrayed her! How could I be so disloyal? I'd tried to answer the questions as honestly as I could, but I didn't expect them to be interpreted like this!

"Your mother was in a lot of pain, Wynford." Joe continued in a quieter voice. "Didn't you ever wonder why that was? Didn't you ever think what caused her heartache?"

"What heartache?" I said, in a resentful tone. "My mother never suffered from any heartache!"

He paused and looked me straight in the eye ... "Didn't she?"

I broke down in tears and cried like a baby. Deep down I'd known the truth all along, but had been too afraid to confront it. These tears were for Mam – her illness, her pain, her suffering. Mam, the person I loved dearly. Then I turned on my father.

"Why didn't my father try to stop her taking those sleeping tablets, Joe? And the laxatives that killed her? Couldn't he see what they were doing to her?"

Joe leaned forward and gently held my arm.

"Could your father have stopped you drinking, Wynford?"

Those words triggered a bizarre reaction. I had a strange vision in which my mother and father were reaching towards me, from beyond the grave, and in doing so they seemed to open my eyes to see them, and myself, in a different perspective. The lingering strands of 'denial' which had fettered me so stubbornly were finally broken and I could now see the addiction for what it really was – an illness. My mother's addiction was an illness, and she could do nothing about it. The same was true of my addiction – an illness that was beyond my control; an illness with its own symptoms, like any other illness – blackouts and denial, to name but two. I calmed myself and sat quietly for a while. Then we both got up and as I thanked him, Joe hugged me and said: "Wynford. If the World Health Organisation can accept the illness concept of alcoholism, perhaps you, too, can accept it now."

Yes, I could. Thanks to Mam, I could. The feeling of relief was intense – like being released from long-term incarceration – free, at last, to do something positive with my life; to take control. I spent some time in the garden that afternoon and experienced a tranquillity I'd never felt before. My head had always been full of clamour and my mind uneasy and discontented. That afternoon my senses were awakened to the wonder of nature – the sounds, the smells, the calm beauty; the world was at peace with me and I was at peace with myself. Free, at last, and empowered to enjoy the gift of life – and all because of my mother, her suffering, and her love.

The most noticeable change in my life was the silencing of the dragon. Since then, I haven't heard that disparaging voice of self-doubt and self-hate that used to depress me so much. I'm always 'on alert', as it were, in case it begins to stir again but, so far, it's been quite dormant. I'm convinced that this has come about because of my mother's intervention, through that vision, in my recovery process. That was the key that opened the door to a new life for me. Once I saw the illness in my mother, I saw the illness in me.

As a result of all this positiveness I began to relax physically, too. I was all arms and legs, like a big spider, sprawled over any chair that was available! But, for some reason, I still had the pain in my stomach. One day Joe called me to his room and told me he wanted me to 'ventilate' – a well-tried method, he maintained, of dealing with unresolved anger. He told me to think of someone I disliked. I had plenty of choice! Then he told me to stand in front of the open window and shout at this person as if he or she were the other end of the field. I could use any sound, but not words, and the sound had to come from the stomach (where anger is harboured) and not the solar plexus (where hatred resides). I did this for about ten minutes and, sure enough, something gave way inside me. I began to cry profusely, without knowing why and, miraculously, the tension and the pain in my stomach began to ease.

Apparently, the stomach pain I'd suffered for years had been caused by a failure to deal appropriately with anger. It all stemmed from my eagerness to please – to be liked by people. Instead of giving vent to my anger towards people, I would bottle it up inside me and pretend there was nothing wrong. I didn't have an ulcer after all, just a case of emotional indigestion! Ventilating gradually eased these tensions and, as the weeks went by, my stomach pains disappeared. Today, the condition of my stomach is like an early warning system. If my recovery programme is in danger of being sidetracked, or if I'm not being entirely honest about my feelings, I'm alerted by painful twinges. But as long as I'm sober, in spirit, mind and body, my stomach is fine.

There's no doubt that the root cause of much of the violent behaviour in our society today is the inability to deal appropriately with pent-up emotion, be it anger or jealousy or whatever. My method of dealing with the resulting tension was to disappear into my bottle of alcohol. Unfortunately, that is the all-too-easy answer for so many people – alcohol, or drugs, or other forms of addiction – and the all-too-familiar result is domestic and social violence. If only – and it's a massive 'if' – if only the sufferers could be given some help to come to terms with their own emotions, to develop self-esteem and self-respect!

I can only speak for myself but I know that the turn-around in my life was only possible through a spiritual experience. That evening outside the off-licence when I realised, and accepted, that alcohol had had the better of me, I had a clear vision that it was my suffering over all the previous years that had brought me to that point – the point when I was prepared to change my behaviour and prepared to reach out for help in order to achieve that change. During the previous twenty-six years I had tried several times to turn my back on alcohol, but it was a hopeless cause. I was powerless to fight against it. My spiritual experience showed me that if

I was to recover and live a sober life, I had to find another power. And that was the message rammed home at Rhoserchan – find another power, or die.

The 'other power', or the 'higher power', can take many different forms but, given my background as the son of the manse, I suppose it was odds-on that the 'higher power' that would offer itself to me was the Christian God – not the God of revenge that is found in the Old Testament, but the God of love and forgiveness found in the New Testament. The platform was already there; it was just a case of yielding to it – allowing it into my life to do its work. No, it was more than that; it was *wanting* it to work. The *desire* has to be there.

Although the idea of yielding to a 'higher power' had been in my mind for some time, the act itself was a conscious decision – and a tentative one at that! In essence, I was prepared to take a gamble on God because I had nothing to lose! One afternoon, I went with a friend (himself a believer) to a quiet corner of the garden at Rhoserchan and there, beside the stream, I knelt and prayed. I prayed for deliverance from my captivity, and I prayed for guidance and strength to do His will on earth.

The words came easily and, I must admit, I was expecting immediate results! But nothing dramatic happened; the heavens didn't open and no dove came to land on my shoulder! My friend warned me that I had to be more patient – to give time, time. But he also reminded me that I hadn't drunk alcohol for several weeks, so there was something going on inside me. He promised me that if I kept my faith I would definitely see a difference. I believed him. Drinking again was not an option.

Meira and the girls came to visit me for two hours every Sunday afternoon. This was my only contact with the outside world; daily papers were not allowed, the TV was hardly ever switched on, and listening to the *Top Twenty* programme on the radio on Sunday evening was our only entertainment. These family visits were of great value and importance. They offered an opportunity for us as a family to learn more about the illness – the illness which affected all of us and in which we were all enmeshed – and there were opportunities to build bridges.

During these visits there would be various presentations – talks or videos – and there was always a counsellor at hand to offer support and advice. We also had private time together and sometimes, while Bethan and Rwth played in the garden, Meira and I would have some precious moments together, alone.

The alcoholic's recovery period can be difficult for the whole family. The change in what has become 'accepted' or 'expected' behaviour can cause considerable strain and stress. It's important, then, that the whole family unit is involved – that they go through the recovery process together, accepting that each family member, albeit inadvertently, has played some part in causing and maintaining the illness. Each family member, therefore, needs to recognise and acknowledge his or her need for help if they want to be free of their obsession with alcohol and with the alcoholic.

That is why Al-Anon and Alateen, self-help support groups for friends and relatives of alcoholics, are so important. During my period at Rhoserchan, Meira attended Al-Anon meetings and the girls went to Alateen. Thankfully, the Ellis

Owen family, together, was putting the illness behind it.

My next task was to prepare a fearless and thorough moral self-assessment – to write up an in-depth and totally honest inventory of my own personality. I wrote about all the character defects that had made me turn to drink: fear, pride, self-pity, cowardice, being self-opinionated, criticising others, bad temper, rage, deceit, jealousy, feelings of guilt, negativity – the list went on and on. I had to write about how each one of my failings had affected my life and my relationship with others. Then I had to turn them all into positive features, such as forgiveness, courage, humility, honesty, love, tolerance, trust, positiveness – all of which would provide a platform for sustained recovery.

It was a painful experience – in the same way as writing this book has been a painful experience – but cathartic. It enabled me to take responsibility for my actions in the past, and to firmly shut the door on them. What was done was done; I came to terms with it and the feelings of guilt and shame were banished for good.

But there was one final step to take before the process ended – I had to present my self-assessment to another person – a complete stranger, in my case. So, on my last Thursday afternoon at Rhoserchan, I went to meet this person in a small room, fully aware of the fact that I had to be completely open with this stranger – and also conscious of the need to be on the level with the 'higher power' in my life, my God.

I started rather nervously, half expecting him to frown in disgust at some of my confessions. But instead, he showed complete empathy! "Yea! Been there, done that!" And from there on we spoke the same language, as it were. I wasn't alone any more! Sharing my experiences with this other person, divulging my innermost feelings and thoughts to him, and being conscious that I was doing so in the presence of my God, was nothing less than a blessing. I came out of that room a new man. The old shackles had gone. A new life was beckoning!

On the 24th of October 1992, Meira, Bethan and Rwth came to take me home in the car. It was, obviously, a joyous occasion. As we travelled towards Cardiff it began to dawn on me how much protection and security the centre had given me over the past three months. Would I be able to survive in the real world without that support? How would I begin to face the many people I'd offended or let down? What about my overdraft? Would I get a job? How would we cope with Christmas...? Then a voice whispered to me, clearly and firmly: "Hey! Wynford! Get a grip! One day at a time!" Yes, I couldn't agree more!

RECOVERY

...the success I'd been enjoying
recently had happened, not in spite of
the fact that I was an alcoholic, but
because I was an alcoholic – and
because I'd accepted help...

The phrase 'One day at a time!' was to become my motto, eventually. But for the first few months of my sobriety I expected everything to fall into place straight away. I expected to pick up my career where I'd left it, paying off my debt would be no problem, and making amends to all the people I'd offended would be an easy matter. How wrong I was! The analogy with a heavy tanker heading full speed towards the rocks is a bit of a cliché, but it's quite apt. The engines can be put in reverse but the ship will still head towards the rocks for some time. I was doing all the right things – the necessary things – working on changing my behaviour and attitude, and helping others, but my life was still on course for disaster. On the jobs front nothing happened and my debt grew and grew. (In fact, in the first three years of being sober my debt almost trebled to thirty thousand pounds, forcing me to re-mortgage the house. It was a nightmare.) In the meantime I'd found a sponsor, Bryn, himself a recovering alcoholic, who offered me advice and support, and did everything he could to help me. It was he who kept me on track, constantly reminding me that in order to stay sober a recovering alcoholic must possess two virtues – patience and faith. And by staying sober, he promised, my patience and faith would be rewarded, eventually.

As well as my career and the debt, I had other pressing matters to which I had to attend. My relationship with Meira and the girls being one of them. My main role here was that of listening – listening to *their* side of the story, without justifying my behaviour. To be reminded of all the terrible things I had done to them was a painful experience but, gradually, as Meira, Bethan and Rwth opened their hearts and vented their revulsion and bitterness, very gradually, washed in tears of remorse and forgiveness, the wounds began to heal.

It took nine years for me to fully regain their trust and, in a way, I'm glad it took so long. The harder the struggle to achieve something, the more it is valued, and that trust means everything to me. And it was a struggle. Meira worked extremely hard to keep the family together; and I think I did my bit too, with my faith in my God giving me strength in my hours of need. It was a period of healing of body and mind, but most important of all, it was a period when I grew and matured spiritually. The constant effort to keep that trust is now part and parcel of my sobriety – one day at a time.

Another painful experience, and an inevitable part of the process, was confronting the other woman. She came to see me one day when I was at Bryn's house in Cowbridge. She couldn't control her anger towards me and she physically assaulted me. I couldn't reason with her, or try to explain anything – or even say how sorry I was for deceiving her with my false promises. Her feelings had been too deeply hurt for that. I've been told that the only way to deal with that kind of situation is to stay completely out of the person's life. That I have done, but the affair has left a bruise on my heart that is a constant reminder of how destructive the illness can be.

But there were ups as well as downs, and two examples shine like beacons in my memory. Rwth had booked a skiing holiday with the school and had been looking forward to the trip with great excitement. That's all she'd been talking about for weeks! The night before they were due to leave, however, as she was having a bath and chatting to Meira, she began to cry uncontrollably. When I went upstairs to see what was going on, she sobbed: "I don't want to go skiing tomorrow, Dad – not now that you're better!" Shortly afterwards Bethan hugged me and said: "Dad. I'm so, so proud of you!"

To say that I was uplifted is an understatement. Those words meant so much to me! Bryn, my sponsor, had told me that by staying sober and by maturing spiritually, I could live a most wonderful life. I had just been given a vital injection of hope!

And there were other signs of goodwill towards me during those apprehensive days. Both Equity and the Writers' Guild offered me financial assistance – a sum of two and a half thousand pounds each – which was gratefully accepted. This token of friendship and support was all the more meaningful because it came from establishments that represented my colleagues – many of whom I had maligned and vilified during my illness years. I was humbled by their kindness and, as a result, I vowed to take a more active interest in the union's affairs when the opportunity arose. In a few years' time I was elected to the Welsh National Committee of Equity, and later became its Chairman, a position I held with great pride for several years.

Although the donation from the two unions had considerably eased my financial situation, I still suffered from 'fear of financial insecurity'. This is a condition that afflicts all alcoholics as they begin to recover. It doesn't matter how poor or, indeed, how rich they are – they all go through the same pangs of fear of financial insecurity. And learning how to handle this fear is part of the recovery process. Basically, that means adjusting their sense of values so that money and material belongings come very low on the list of priorities in life. Easier said than done, perhaps! In my case, coping with my debt made that adjustment a little easier.

I had to face up to the possibility of being declared bankrupt – and all the stigma attached to that. What would people say? It would be a devastating blow to me and the family! Or ... would it, really? It was Bryn who helped me realise how groundless this fear was. We discussed values and priorities, and I came to the conclusion that even bankruptcy would not be the end of the world – as long as I stayed sober. That was the key. As long as I was sober there was hope that I could do something about my problem. It didn't matter what some people might say or do to me, nothing could hurt me any more – as long as I was sober. Sobriety emerged as the one thing that really mattered in my life – more important than my relationship with Meira, more important than my love for my own two daughters even – because I knew that if I were to drink again I would lose everything! Fortified by this realisation, I was able to overcome my fear of financial insecurity once and for all.

Timing is everything, they say. I was glad that the cheque for twenty thousand pounds didn't arrive before I'd firmly established the importance of my sobriety. Otherwise it might have interfered with the process. I'd completely forgotten about the life insurance policy that was about to mature, and when it arrived, it came as a very welcome surprise. But the euphoria didn't last for long. One would have expected me to be on top of the world now that my financial worries were more or less over and the path ahead firmly mapped out. But no; I was still in the doldrums, miserable as anything, because I now realised that financial insecurity was only one of a host of other fears. My mind was a jumble of conflicting insecurities – afraid of failure, afraid of success, afraid of even trying. Afraid of meeting people, afraid of expressing an opinion, afraid of being open about my feelings.

It was Bryn, again, who put his finger on the problem. Having a negative attitude had become ingrained in me, always allowing the problem to dominate over any thoughts of a solution. He pointed out that these unfounded fears of mine were threatening to stifle my hopes of recovery by preventing me from making a positive contribution to life. He said that having faith in a 'higher power', God in my case, didn't mean I could leave everything to Him and neglect my own contribution to the recovery. I had to make an effort, too! This is when I realised that God wouldn't do for me what I could do for myself. I had to co-operate with my 'higher power'.

I approached the challenge in two ways. The first was to make a list of the fears that were bugging me. For example:

Fear of speaking in a meeting.

Why? The last time I did it I made a fool of myself and my opinion was ignored.

Then I made a note of how it affected me – my emotional and financial security, my self-esteem, my relationship with others, my personal and social ambitions, etc.. Then I looked at what I might have done to cause that fear in the first place; had I been selfish or self-seeking, had I been dishonest, irrational, or flippant, and so on. Finally, I tried to think of ways to ensure the same thing wouldn't happen again – to think and behave differently. Oh, yes! There was one further step – not a written exercise this time! Having considered the 'evidence' and decided on a plan of action to deal with each fear, I then turned to my God and offered a humble prayer for strength and courage to carry out my intentions. I found it worked wonders for me.

The second approach was more direct – and quicker. With some of the fears I just took them as a challenge – head on – conscious of the fear, but pressing ahead anyway! By now I tend to use fear as a reason to do things rather than as an excuse not to. (FEAR: Face Everything And Recover.) But I think this confidence is based on the spiritual development I gained by going through the process of analysing the fears, working out a solution, and deriving courage from the 'higher power' in my life.

Gradually, one day at a time, I was able to overcome my fears. But even then, I still suffered from the 'negativity' that was so ingrained in me. I used to wake up in the morning with a feeling of impending doom and thinking what might go wrong that day. This wasn't the kind of life I had expected to enjoy in sobriety. This is when I began to use 'positive affirmations' as a means of changing my outlook on life. I'd get up in the morning and write phrases in my notebook, such as: 'I have good health, vitality and prosperity'; 'I solve all my problems'; 'I have enough money not to have to worry about money'; 'I keep my life simple, and trust absolutely'. It was important that some of these affirmations were to do with spiritual values, for example, 'I am at peace with myself and my fellow man'; 'If God is for me, who can be against me'; 'God will provide for me and care for me in every way, at every moment'. Then, every single night and morning, I'd read these affirmations to myself and reflect on how good life really was. It's amazing how the human mind responds to such positive prompting!

I'd set myself realistic, achievable goals, too, and although I'd accepted the fact that money wasn't the most important thing in life, bills still had to be paid, so many of my goals were quite materialistic – to do with my career and my salary!

My career development during this period can only be described as 'halting'. I'd have a job for a month or two, and then five months of kicking my heels. Two steps forward and five back! It was a testing time and we relied heavily on Meira's income. There was one significant development, however. Early in 1994, my colleague and friend, John Pierce Jones, and I were commissioned by S4C to write a children's comedy series. Although the work was completed, it was never filmed due to a change of personnel at S4C. But we did get as far as appointing an independent production company. Two companies were short-listed – Cwmni Teledu Elidir (Elidir Television Company), run by Emlyn Davies who, you may recall, had been fairly high up on my 'hate list' of old, and Cambrensis, a company run by my brother, Arwel. It was a tough call – two excellent bids and, of course, there was the small matter of brotherly loyalty – but in the end we went for Elidir.

Arwel was visibly disappointed. But to be perfectly honest, Elidir had a good track record in drama production, and Cambrensis had none. John was firmly in favour of Elidir and I went along with that. I must confess that I was slightly swayed by a feeling of wanting to 'make amends' to Emlyn Davies for what had happened between us previously. But it was the right decision professionally – and it had far-reaching implications for my relationship with Arwel. If we, as brothers, were to work together professionally in the future, as was my genuine wish, there would have to be a change of attitude between us. I would have to rid myself of the secret jealousy that I'd always harboured towards Arwel and his amazing professional achievements, and he would have to forget those 'pigeonholes' that we had been put into in our childhood days – where Arwel was labelled the academic and me the comedian. From now on I didn't want to be seen only as fit for 'light relief' – we had to be on equal terms. How this was to come about, I had no idea. I accepted that the biggest change had to take place within my own mind and I made a conscious effort to achieve that. It took time and effort and I relied greatly on deriving strength from my 'higher power' to help me in the process. Initially, there was a sense of coldness and detachment between us, but gradually we came together on a new footing and our relationship developed into true brotherly love. It's a wonderful feeling.

Fairly soon after that, work began to pick up. In June 1994, Opus Television Company offered me a small part in a TV series called *Halen yn y Gwaed* (Salt in the Blood), which involved a week's work in Ireland. Also, I was given a part in the National Eisteddfod play which would be staged at Neath later that year (August 1994). I remember the audition well. Tim Baker, the director, asked me: "Wynford. Can you give me a guarantee that you won't drink tomorrow?" My quick reply was: "Only if you can give me your guarantee, Tim, that you will still be alive this time tomorrow!" It may have sounded flippant, but it summed up my 'one day at a time' philosophy perfectly. He got my meaning. "Touché!" he said, and offered me the part. Knowing that I had this job lined up gave me a lot of confidence.

During that period of making positive affirmations and setting realistic and achievable goals, I used to say to myself that I couldn't think of anything that would make me start drinking again – unless, perhaps, if something were to happen to one of the girls. It's dangerous to attach any conditions to such vows because, sure enough, you will be tested sooner or later. My test came on the 18th of June 1994. It was a Saturday night and Bethan had gone to town with her friends. I was preparing to sail to Ireland the following morning to do some filming for Opus. The telephone rang. It was the police. "It's nothing to worry about, but your daughter's been involved in an accident. Could you please come straight down to the Infirmary?" When we got to A&E, Bethan's friends were there, safe and unhurt, but there was no sign of Bethan. We were informed that the Fire Brigade were still working on getting her out of the back seat of the car, where she had been crushed. She eventually arrived, strapped to a stretcher so that she couldn't move an inch. She had a broken back and a nasty fracture of the right leg. We were shocked. Devastated! But we consoled each other by saying it could have been worse. At least she was alive, and conscious. We thanked God and offered a silent prayer.

I don't know what possessed me to carry on with my trip to Ireland the following day. I rang the hospital first thing in the morning and they said she'd had a fairly comfortable night. They'd be operating on her during the day and assured me that everything would be OK. If I were in that situation today I wouldn't have gone, but at the time I was still in that immature phase of 'people-pleasing' – wanting to be liked, I suppose. As we sailed out of Fishguard that day my mind was back in Cardiff. I couldn't concentrate on any conversation, so I left the film crew and went to the top deck to find some solitude. And there, deep in thought, I heard a voice speaking to me, saying all would be well, that I should look after myself, and that I should go to a fellowship meeting once I'd arrived in Ireland to seek the support of other recovering alcoholics. This made me feel better and, again, I shut my eyes and prayed for Bethan.

A few weeks later I was performing in the Eisteddfod play at the town hall in Neath. And Bethan was performing in the Eisteddfod pavilion, on crutches, winning the prestigious Richard Burton Prize for the best actor!

This was the beginning of a good spell. John Pierce Jones and I were commissioned to script a BBC Radio Cymru (Wales) comedy series – which proved to be very popular. I was also offered a part in a TV series which was destined for a long run, and I performed in two pantomimes. The steady income enabled me to finally pay off my debt to Arwel and Rowenna.

Towards the end of 1995, Graham Laker offered me a part in a play he was staging at Theatr Gwynedd in Bangor. This turned out to be a fateful event – not for any reason to do with the production or the performance, but because this was when I discovered a book that was to transform my whole life.

During a break in rehearsals I went to the public library in Bangor and found a brown-covered, bland-looking volume about the life and doctrines of Meister Eckhart (c1260 – 1327), a Dominican friar and German philosopher, a spiritual psychologist, who was renowned for his preaching to lay people about his vision of the relationship between man and God. His central theme was 'the presence of God in the individual soul, and the dignity of the soul of the just man'. What attracted me to that particular book I do not know! But as soon as I started reading it, I was fascinated. I was excited, even, because I sensed he had a message for me, personally! And, indeed, he did. By reading that book I learned so many things about God – things that were to become the very foundation of my view of life.

In essence, I learned that I could have a direct relationship with God, one to one, and also that he was available where and when I needed him. I could even catch him in his kitchen if I wanted to. This was the kind of relationship I needed with my 'higher power', because I didn't know when or where I'd next be tempted to drink. Whenever that might be, I'd need instant access to his help. From then on it became my main objective in life to improve my understanding of God and to deepen my relationship with Him. That, and maintaining my sobriety – because, in effect, they mean the same thing. I now believe in God absolutely; I have every faith that he will provide for me, my real needs, always.

A few years later, I went to a worldwide convention for alcoholics in Minneapolis, USA. On the Saturday night, instead of joining the thousands gathered in the Edgar Hoover Convention Centre, I went with a friend to a Roman Catholic cathedral in nearby St. Paul's. The theme of the priest's address was 'faith', as exemplified by the woman who touched the cloak of Jesus and was healed from her haemorrhaging. He compared her faith to that of the recovering alcoholic, and he said these words: "We in the church believe God exists. Alcoholics – and there are eighty thousand of them in Minneapolis this evening – they *know* he exists!" I was one of the eighty thousand, and the priest's words were certainly true of me.

Forgiving, and accepting forgiveness, are important aspects of the Christian faith. In a similar way, making amends to the people who have been hurt is a very important part of any alcoholic's recovery. And making amends to those who have died is just as important as with those who are still alive. Mam and Dad were on my list, and R. H. Pritchard-Jones, the headmaster who had been top of my hate list for so many years. It wasn't easy in his case, because the feelings I harboured towards him were still very negative. That had to change before I could make any progress, so I began to pray for him – for his soul to be blessed with everlasting peace and happiness. But I must confess that my prayers, at first, were not entirely sincere, and were said through gritted teeth!

However, after about a month of praying I began to feel better towards him. I saw our relationship in a different light. What had happened between us began to appear as a misunderstanding, or misinterpretation, and we arrived at a mutual forgiveness. Only then could I begin to make amends to him properly. I wrote him a letter apologising for my behaviour in school and for my offensive attitude towards him, and my defiance. Then I held a little ceremony in the garden to burn the letter, offering a short prayer. And that was it! All the malice I'd harboured for years just left me; the sense of relief was amazing. I can honestly say that the spiritual relationship I now have with my former headmaster, the man I used to hate with a passion, is one of love and respect. The inner peace that came with this was achieved through prayer, and with the grace of God.

I went through the same kind of process with my parents – even the burning of a letter – revisiting many unpleasant situations in our past and facing up to some painful truths. Gradually, I was able to exorcise the anger I had felt towards them as I grew up in the manse – the misplaced anger of a young man who felt that his mother was using her illness to control him, and that his father was placing too high an expectation on him, forcing him to be a person other than his true self. As I honestly re-lived these experiences I came to realise that their motives were entirely natural; they were only doing their best for me under very difficult circumstances. Once I saw our relationship in that light, I was overwhelmed by a feeling of compassion, love and respect. I am now at peace with Mam and Dad and I've taken them down from the pedestal on which I'd once placed them.

It was the same process, more or less, with people who were still alive – except there was the extra step of actually meeting them, face to face. I don't think this took more courage, only that the timing had to be spot on. In the case of Emlyn Davies, for example, the S4C executive whom I'd resented for so long, I tried several times to take advantage of a chance meeting with him – we both had a lot of social interests in common – to apologise and make amends. But something always happened to interrupt. Somebody would join us in our conversation, or perhaps he'd have to rush off somewhere. It was as if I wasn't meant to do it at that particular moment. The fact was that I wasn't spiritually ready for it – I still hadn't rid myself completely of the old animosity within me, and wasn't yet willing to make amends to him. However, when the opportunity finally came and I was able to ask for his forgiveness, he said that he bore no malice or ill will towards me; that he had never done so, and that there was nothing to forgive.

And that should have been the end of the matter. But no! Although I had made amends to Emlyn, my feelings towards him had not really changed. This bothered me a lot because I'd expected to feel the same kind of warmth that I'd felt towards my parents and my former headmaster. There was something seriously wrong with my recovery, I thought. Bryn suggested that I should give myself permission not to like him. He explained that I didn't have to like everybody – that it was possible to love people without necessarily liking them! This wasn't an easy concept to grasp, but as soon as I understood the difference, and accepted it, all the ill feeling I bore towards Emlyn dropped off my shoulders like a heavy mantle. It was that sudden – and that wonderful!

What I had done, of course, was to accept the situation – and 'acceptance is the answer to all our problems'! With time, I grew to like Emlyn as a person and by now we have become good friends.

I soon realised that the process of making amends was a slow one. I had to learn to be very patient and to prepare myself meticulously, both mentally and spiritually, before making the approach. One by one, however, and one day at a time, I was eventually reconciled to all my imagined 'enemies'. The purge is complete, and now that I have nothing to hide from myself or anyone else, I am able to turn to my God with an open heart and receptive mind to seek his guidance in all that I do. In the prologue to this book I mentioned that when I feel the need to meditate, I have a heavenly garden which I visit in my imagination. All my departed friends are gathered there, and there I have direct contact with my God. I visit that garden quite often – it is my main source of solace and strength.

Having been a public figure for some time I suppose it was only natural that there would be a public interest in my private life as a recovering alcoholic. Llinos Wyn, a BBC producer, approached me to invite us as a family to take part in a Radio Cymru (Wales) documentary on alcoholism. I, personally, had no objection, and neither did Bethan or Rwth. Meira, however, was rather reticent. She was worried about the possible adverse effect on her position as an Infants teacher in the school. How would the parents react to the knowledge that their child's teacher was married to an alcoholic? These very thoughts, of course, reflected the social stigma attached to alcoholism. There was no way we could go ahead with the programme without Meira's contribution, so that was that.

There was no further discussion until one day Meira said she'd had second thoughts. She'd come to the conclusion that by not taking part she was actually helping to maintain the stigma and the prejudice people had towards alcoholics. Her wish, now, was to speak openly and honestly about what had happened to our family in the hope that, by doing so, she might help others realise there was a way out of the illness; that there was hope to repair the damage and regain happiness.

After the recording – each one of us separately – there was very little discussion of what had been said, only a general consensus that we'd been perfectly honest. When the tape of the programme arrived by post one day, we were all rather apprehensive. We went to the bedroom to listen to it. No one said a word, but at the end we were all in tears, hugging each other. We were so glad that we'd done it. A heavy cloud of guilt and shame had been dispersed and we felt we could now walk with our heads held high.

The key element in the process of recovery is honesty – and it may be difficult for some members of the extended family to accept the home truths. To their credit, Arwel and Rowenna, my brother and sister, reacted positively to the programme when it was later broadcast. Their support has been important to us, as a family, in our recovery.

There followed four years of non-stop examinations in our house. Bethan and Rwth worked hard at their 'A' Levels and GCSEs and were rewarded with success – Bethan becoming a student at the Royal Welsh College of Music and Drama, my old college, and Rwth going to the University of Wales College of Medicine, Cardiff. I can claim no part in their success but at least, now that I was sober, I didn't cause them any distraction from their studies.

It is a sad fact that alcoholism is a hereditary illness. Alcoholics are usually aware of this, and keep an eye out for any telltale signs, but there isn't much they can do about it. Whilst at college Bethan suffered from acute bulimia and had to attend TUKES, the treatment centre for emotional and addictive illnesses in Aberystwyth. She came through it, thank God, and today lives a perfectly healthy life. She is married, with two children – Begw Non and Efa Grug – whom Meira and I regard as the world's greatest treasures. They have given our lives a new dimension. We can only hope that our grandchildren will not be affected by our family illness. But if they are, there is real hope that they may find a way to overcome the problem. If Bethan and I have done so, with God's help, living one day at a time, then it should also be possible for others.

1997 and 1998 were good years for me professionally. To begin with, Arwel gave me a huge confidence boost when he drew my attention to a European-wide competition to write a children's play for television, and suggested that I should have a go. I discussed some potential themes with him, including one based on my own childhood antics, and he thought the story about the pork pie was particularly apt. That was when I dissected a pork pie, took out the filling to make a sandwich, and put the pie back in the pantry. The next day, after Mam had complained to the factory about a 'faulty pie', we had a visit from the Manager, who apologised and offered us a hamper of food in compensation! The script came to me quite easily; I gave it the title *Porc Pei* and sent it off to the competition, quietly confident that I had as good a chance of success as any other contender!

Then Arwel offered me some scripting and acting roles in two documentaries that he was producing with his company, Cambrensis. My long-held ambition to work with Arwel was beginning to be realised, and this gave me great satisfaction.

Other career developments quickly followed, including working with Theatr Gwynedd on a new and modern production of *Siwan* by Saunders Lewis, with a successful short tour of Wales.

During this period Arwel invited Meira and me to the Welsh BAFTA Awards dinner and I remember how we were able to enjoy the evening – free of any inhibitions, but on guard! People often ask me how I can enjoy such social occasions when alcohol is freely flowing. The answer is to be prepared and to be constantly on guard. In the first place, I must make sure that I go there for the right reason. Then I make sure I have an escape plan in case I feel uncomfortable and want to leave early. That means I always drive the car – I don't depend on anyone else for a lift. Then I take meticulous care with my drinks – I don't accept any drink without seeing it being poured, and I never leave my glass out of my sight. I also avoid any food that contains alcohol. I know that a quarter of an eggcup of alcohol would kill me. This list of 'dos' and 'don'ts' sounds a bit of a drag, but by now they are second nature to me.

But I stray from the BAFTA event, which was memorable also for another reason – a chance meeting during the interval with Meirion Davies, the then Commissioner of Children's Programmes with S4C. He was very interested in how I'd come to write the play *Porc Pei* for the European competition – something that had gone completely out of my mind! It turned out that he was one of the adjudicators, and he confided in me that *Porc Pei* had reached the short list of three but that it had not been awarded the prize for 'political' reasons. He strongly suggested that I should submit the script to S4C – hinting that I could possibly be commissioned to turn it into a film.

By strange coincidence, the formal commission arrived at the same time as Angharad Jones* was appointed Drama Commissioner for S4C. In the meantime I'd received a commission to write a play for Theatr Powys. It never rains but pours!

The commission from S4C was to create a film for family viewing on Christmas Eve. Being that it would be based on a script I had already written I thought it would be a dawdle. But I completely lost the plot! I turned it into a grand tragedy, with the hero committing suicide by swallowing his mother's sleeping tablets! (Cathartic strains emerging?) Drama Commissioner Angharad Jones condemned the script as totally unsuitable for a Christmas Eve family viewing, and suggested I went back to the drawing board. I started from scratch, took a completely different tack, turned it into a comedy, and convinced myself I had a winner. Not so. It didn't fare any better than the first draft. At the meeting with Angharad Jones and the scripts editor, the script was rubbished and I left with Angharad's words ringing in my ears: "Everything must revolve around the pork pie, Wynford!"

I felt quite disheartened and decided to concentrate, instead, on the Theatr Powys commission. That's how *Gwin Coch a Fodca* (Red Wine and Vodka) came to be written – a play based on my own desperate journey into the clutches of alcoholism and drug-abuse. For twenty-six years, Meic, the main character, has been a slave to alcohol and other drugs.

---

* *Angharad Jones died in tragic circumstances in January 2010.*

It is a raw and revealing play, which follows Meic's twisted thoughts and irrational behaviour that held him in the throes of the sickness for so long, and brought him to within a whisker of losing everything.

I thought Theatr Powys were very brave to offer me the commission in the first place, but when I began discussing the theme with them, they were so supportive. Their attitude towards alcoholism was so positive and they were really keen to learn more about the condition. I felt greatly encouraged and inspired. On this occasion, the script seemed to flow from my pen – or from my fingertips, to be technologically precise! The exercise had a strong element of catharsis, naturally, and I wondered how people might react to the raw truth – especially Arwel and Rowenna. But, as I said before, by that stage in my life I used any 'fear' as an incentive to do things, rather than an excuse not to.

If you remember, my colleague and friend, Mici Plwm, was another person I'd offended at one time. Well, this was an opportunity to make amends to him. I was able to ensure that the job of producing *Gwin Coch a Fodca* was given to him – a gesture I know he appreciated – and it was a job well done. In the audience on the first night at the Wyeside Arts Centre in Builth Wells on the 10th of July 1998, were Arwel and Rowenna, my old friend, Merêd, and some of the staff of Rhoserchan. To my relief, the response was favourable. It had a similar response during the ensuing tour – well attended, well received, although a few critics maintained it wasn't a real play, in the traditional sense. Perhaps so. But what was important to me was the fact that I'd been able to provide some enlightenment and generate some debate on the taboo subject of alcoholism.

Radio Cymru (Wales) producer, Aled Jones, invited me to make a radio adaptation of the play, which was broadcast on Sunday evening, the 11th of October, 1998. I was grateful to him for the opportunity to get the message across to a wider audience.

As time went by, I gave up on the idea of completing the *Porc Pei* film script for S4C. Then, one day, as Meira and I were travelling towards Fishguard, we stopped at a pub for a coffee. Suddenly, ideas for the film started to fill my mind and Meira and I jotted them down like mad on beer mats! It was unbelievable! By the time we left the pub, half an hour later, the plot was complete and every character in place. It still needed the final touches, but within a week the final script was ready to hand in. This time, Angharad Jones was more than pleased. She thought it was great.

Strange as it may seem, I was convinced that my writing of that script was inspired by my 'higher power'. And that experience has influenced my way of working ever since. Nowadays, when I start writing on a Monday morning, I co-operate with my 'higher power' – I think of various ideas, turn them over in my head and, gradually, I feel drawn to a certain theme and the words begin to flow. Invariably, by the Tuesday afternoon, the script is ready for typing. It's uncanny – but it works!

So! Work began on the filming of *Porc Pei*. Cambrensis got the film commission, and we were fortunate enough to have the services of Paul Turner as director (he was already well-known for his award-winning film, *Hedd Wyn*,* in 1992) and Siân Davies as producer. But what gave me the greatest thrill was working again with Arwel – on a really big project this time.

The film was completed in twelve days. At the end of each day's shooting I was invited to view the 'rushes', i.e. the result of the previous day's filming. I didn't really want to see these, but on one occasion I accepted. On the way to the editing suite, I stopped to question why I had changed my mind. The only thing that was different on this occasion was that Angharad Jones, the Drama Commissioner, would be present. I knew the film was good, and I knew that Angharad would compliment me – and I realised that my true motive was nothing to do with viewing the rushes! I took the next turning towards Dinas Dinlle and spent the rest of the evening walking my favourite beach.

The alcoholics' ego is a dangerous thing – it can easily undermine their efforts to maintain their sobriety. I knew that, and dealing with success was a new challenge for me. I knew I had to hit it on the head. Back home in Cardiff I had plenty of support. If I showed any signs of losing touch with reality, forgetting who and what I was, Meira and the girls would have no qualms in bringing me back to earth. I also had a good circle of friends to whom I could turn for help at any time. And if I needed any additional reminders of what could happen to me if ever I started drinking again, all I had to do was think of the numerous funerals I'd been to – people who

---

* *Hedd Wyn is a 1992 Welsh-language film written by Alan Llwyd and directed by Paul Turner. It won a BAFTA award for the best foreign language film in the year of its release. It was nominated for an Academy Award for Best Foreign Language Film. The film is a biopic based on the life of the legendery Welsh poet Hedd Wyn, who was killed in the First World War and posthumously awarded a Chair at the National Eisteddfod of Wales at Birkenhead in 1917.*

thought they had all the answers; people who thought they didn't need any help.

The film, *Porc Pei*, was well received when it was shown at the Chapter Theatre in Cardiff and at Theatr Gwynedd in Bangor. It also had favourable reviews after it was broadcast on S4C on Christmas Eve, 1998. The pinnacle, though, was being awarded the first prize at the International Film Festival in Würzburg, Germany. Meira and I were there for the occasion. It was a wonderful experience, and I will always remember the thrill of telephoning Arwel to tell him the good news! Our first major venture together – and we had hit the jackpot!

Success breeds success! Early in 1999, I received a further commission from S4C to write a new TV series based on the characters in *Porc Pei*. There was only one possible title for the series – *Porc Peis Bach* (Little Pork Pies)! And there was a bonus, too – Cambrensis was commissioned to produce the series, so the professional partnership with Arwel would continue for some time to come.

1999 was also the year in which I was invited to become a Patron of the Rhoserchan Project – an honour which I was proud to accept. But this was not a coincidence. It came about in order to remind me that all the success I'd been enjoying recently had happened, not in spite of the fact that I was an alcoholic, but *because* I was an alcoholic – and because I'd accepted help. I was filled with a sense of appreciation of what I had received at Rhoserchan. I fully realised the value of that gift of sobriety – and I understood the significance of that realisation. From then on, my main purpose in life would be to carry the message and help other alcoholics to achieve sobriety.

EPILOGUE

A NEW MILLENNIUM AND A NEW LIFE

Stopping drinking by itself is not
enough. Most alcoholics get into
trouble when they think they only
need help to resolve their
immediate problems with alcohol.
This is only the half of it...

Having enjoyed the benefits of sobriety for ten years, it occurred to me that telling others about my journey from addiction to recovery might be one small way of helping others to achieve the same goal. If I could get well, I thought, with all the problems I had encountered and the depths of despair to which I had plummeted, then anyone could do it.

In 2003, I embarked on the challenge of writing my story* – and a tough challenge it proved to be. The process of writing about my alcoholism was emotionally draining and painful, not just for me but for my wife, Meira, too, because she had been an involuntary participant in the whole insane merry-go-round of my active alcoholism and had suffered dreadfully as a result of my irrational behaviour. Many were the occasions when both of us ended up in tears as we re-lived painful instances when I had placed my need for alcohol above my love for her and our children.

Putting everything down in black and white was, in itself, a cathartic experience and one which helped both Meira and me to come to terms with what had happened. However, we shared the view that there was a greater good at work in the writing of my story. The book was more than an account of my wayward life – it was a book about alcoholism. So much of my behaviour could be described as 'typical' of addicts. In the same way as I was able to identify with the misery and hopelessness of fellow sufferers, I hoped that they could gain hope from my experiences of recovery.

It seems that a number of Welsh speakers have accessed treatment as a result of reading the Welsh book. That, in itself, has made it worthwhile. Hopefully, this book will have a

---

*Raslas bach a mawr! my autobiography in Welsh, was duly published in 2004.

similar effect.

Early in 2004, I completed the script for the final series of *Porc Peis Bach*. The filming of that last series was a joy and a very satisfying conclusion to the whole project. I couldn't have wished for a better ending to one of the most enjoyable, rewarding and creative periods of my life. During that period, however, something happened that was to change my life again and take it in a completely new direction.

One morning, during a break in the filming, I was quietly contemplating the next step in my career when it struck me how much my life had changed since 1992. When I'd stopped drinking, and embarked on the journey of recovery, everything in my life had gradually become positive. My career had been resurrected, my financial worries had been resolved and, more importantly, my relationship with all the people around me had been healed. Furthermore, I felt at one with myself, contented, secure and at ease. I felt so privileged. And in that moment of reflection I decided that I should retire from my career as an actor and writer, and dedicate my time to helping others on the journey to recovery.

At certain stages in my life, I had tried various methods of escaping from the clutches of alcoholism – controlled drinking and other harm-reduction approaches, but to no avail. Then came Rhoserchan, the only centre in Wales that offered a treatment model based on what is known as the Twelve Step Facilitation (TSF)*, which is an adaptation of the abstinence-based 12-Step approach practised by Alcoholics Anonymous. This method requires an acceptance

---

These days most people have heard of this approach due to its prevalence and success (particularly in the USA) in helping people to combat many different sorts of addiction/dependency problems.

that willpower alone is not sufficient to achieve long-term recovery. It all revolves around accepting a 'higher power' as the catalyst for change in one's life.

This was obviously a treatment model that suited me and I left Rhoserchan with a deep sense of indebtedness. But Rhoserchan, near Aberystwyth, was more than a hundred miles from my home and I wondered whether such a distance could be a barrier to some people. It became my ambition, one day, to set up a charity to run a day-care rehabilitation centre in Cardiff that incorporated the TSF approach alongside other effective treatment models and interventions.

That morning during the filming of the final series of *Porc Peis Bach*, it dawned on me that now was the time to make that move. As a first step, though, I felt I needed to become a qualified addictions counsellor. I wrote to Graham Menzies*, who was Programme Co-ordinator at Rhoserchan, to seek his advice on whether or not I was suited to such a role. He invited me to spend a week at the centre in order to find out for myself.

I spent the week observing and contributing to group therapy sessions. I was hooked! By the end of the week I was more determined than ever to become an accredited 'addictions counsellor' and to set up the treatment centre at Cardiff. Graham left me with one final piece of advice: "Get trained at Clouds House in East Knoyle, Wiltshire. You'll receive world-class training there."

****

Graham Clifford Menzies died tragically young in January 2007, a few months after being appointed CEO of Broadway Lodge, the treatment centre in Weston-Super-Mare.

I studied at the Centre of Addictions and Treatment Study (CATS) at Clouds House from October 2006 to 2008, and gained a foundation degree in Addictions Counselling. This has enabled me to become a member of FDAP (the Federation of Drug and Alcohol Professionals). During that very rewarding period at college, not only did I qualify as a counsellor, but I also gained a clearer insight into the nature of the day-care rehabilitation centre I was hoping to set up in Cardiff.

When I began the course, I'd been in recovery for fourteen years. It was a good time to take stock of my situation. What could have been the reason why I'd ended up in such a sorry state?

Firstly, there was the inability to accept myself as I really was. Even as a child, I was not willing to accept the way I felt, the way I thought – the real me. I always wanted to be something I was not. This, and the feeling of being different from other people, caused me great mental and emotional stress and it manifested itself in a combination of a distorted form of arrogance and self-loathing. As I grew up, I felt I was devoid of the qualities that make for meaningful relationships, such as honesty, trust, dependability, hope and love. These are important elements in the make up of the 'complete' person – and these 'spiritual' elements were somehow lacking in my case. All this developed into a sense of unbearable aloneness, a painful emptiness and separation from others, right at the very centre of my being. These were the uncomfortable feelings I was trying to blot out throughout my developing years as I found it difficult to cross the bridge from childhood to adulthood. I tried all kinds of ways of escaping the pain of living – the 'burden of being human' – until, at last, I found alcohol. That proved to be a very effective short cut to feeling good about myself. My problems were over, or so I thought.

This must be a very common experience because in his book, Addiction*, David Marteau, former head of treatment at Clouds House, defines alcoholism and drug addiction as 'the chemical evasion of self'. In other words, using chemicals such as alcohol or other drugs or any 'mood altering' substances to help us be someone other than our true selves.

Being true to oneself, therefore, is the perfect antidote to addiction.

In order to achieve this, however, a major life re-evaluation and re-construction exercise must be undertaken on several levels, including a physical, mental, emotional and spiritual level. Before any of this can take place, the addict must go through the process of admitting and accepting the need for help, and finally asking for it. And the most difficult aspect of the 'help' to understand is the one to do with the 'spiritual' level and accepting the concept of a 'higher power', whatever that may be.

I had underestimated the immense power of alcohol – and its invidiousness. At first it enabled me to do the things that I couldn't do before – by boosting my self-esteem, masking my crippling fears and removing most of my inhibitions. But by the following morning, alarmingly, its effect had dissipated, and I was left feeling worse than before. The only thing I could do was to try and recreate that feel-good factor by drinking more alcohol, and the cycle became

---

Mark Allen Publishing Ltd. 2001.

a pattern of living – a vicious circle. I soon became hooked.

The real cleverness of the illness of alcoholism, however, is that I didn't know that I was in trouble. That's the insanity of it – I was totally incapable of comprehending my true condition. The process by which we continue to believe that alcohol or drugs are our friends, and justify our continued use of them, is called 'denial'. To outsiders and observers it seems glaringly obvious that our lives and the lives of those around us (those who choose to stay, that is) increasingly resemble a battlefield. But we, alcoholics, ask: "What battlefield?"

Then there was the blame culture. I thought that the unmanageability of my life was everyone else's fault. If everybody else stopped doing what they were doing to me, I wouldn't feel the need to drink and take drugs. That illusion had to be smashed – otherwise I'd never get to a stage where I could acknowledge my need for help. But no amount of information about the illness of addiction would remove the denial; no amount of nagging or pleading from my wife and children made the slightest bit of difference. Basically, I was too frightened to confront the painful reality of my condition and denied its very existence by taking more alcohol.

But who is going to be responsible for that 'major life re-evaluation and re-construction exercise' I mentioned earlier? Unfortunately, it is easier said than done. However, unless we take positive steps, suicide can quite often become the easier option, and an increasingly attractive means of escaping the pain. It is a fact that many addicts die or become 'beyond recall' before getting to the point of asking – genuinely asking, that is – for help.

Suffering can be the trigger. And once that happens, it

unleashes other powers that enable us to do things we couldn't do for ourselves, such as stopping drinking or stopping using drugs. The suffering involved in order to get us to that stage is optional. We don't all have to lose everything – health, family, career, sanity, or even our lives. We can access help at any stage of our journey to destruction – provided we are sincere about it. Thankfully, a good counsellor can hasten this process of accepting the need for help through the use of effective interventions.

The implication of this for family members is immense – their responsibility (with counselling support if possible) is to hasten the recognition of the alcoholic's need for help, without forgetting, of course, that they themselves – as evidenced in my own situation – can be part of the problem. They too, therefore, need to change – becoming more vulnerable by showing people who they really are. Paradoxically, they also need to 'toughen up' and, like the alcoholic, recognise that they are, in the main, 'survivors' and not 'victims'.

Stopping drinking by itself is not enough. Most alcoholics get into trouble when they think they only need help to resolve their immediate problems with alcohol. This is only the half of it. I had to accept that my need for help was not a one-off, but ongoing – and that it would have to involve every other aspect of my life as well. The crucial point here is that I accepted the truth – that I, on my own, would never be able to control my drinking over any sustained period of time. I was hard-wired to the allurement of alcohol and, left to my own devices, sooner or later, I would drink alcoholically again. I've attended countless funerals over the years of people who thought they were 'special' and 'different' and who thought they could get away with drinking again. They couldn't. Being 'in recovery' doesn't mean 'recovered'!

Not being able to 'stay stopped' from alcohol or other mood altering substances, and the tendency for cross addiction, is a hugely difficult problem to solve. The preoccupation can manifest itself in a devastating and sometimes uncontrollable urge to once again be in that altered state in which we were once comfortable. It is a mental and emotional aspect of the illness that requires careful handling, with sensitive guidance and strong support. It is not a D.I.Y. job! Addicts have to accept that they simply cannot deal with the situation on their own.

We cannot deny that the recovery process has a spiritual aspect that runs through it all, because without the initial 'hope' and subsequent belief or faith that there might actually be a life beyond addiction, what would be the point of trying? Again, we need help to generate and sustain that all-important 'hope' because, without it, most of us would never get past the first few weeks or months.

So, where is this 'help' going to come from, and what form will it take? If we accept that we, on our own, cannot deal with the problem, it follows that we accept the need for some 'other' power. In the book, I have called it a 'higher power', and it can take many different forms. It can be a religious faith – and there are many of them to choose from – or it can be nature, perhaps, or humanism or, indeed, agnosticism, or even atheism, which is in itself a kind of faith. Very often, however, the 'power' greater than oneself is a group of friends or fellow recovering addicts.

The only thing that matters is the faith you have in that power – the *belief* that it can give you strength; that it can make a difference in your own personal situation. Once we have that *belief*, then spiritual progress begins to take place and we become 'empowered' to take control of our situation and of our lives.

As I was reflecting on what had happened to me, I realised how deeply indebted I was to the help I'd received from other recovering addicts. It seemed to me that another key element in the process of continuing recovery was the sharing of our experiences as we carry the message of hope to others – becoming 'givers' instead of 'takers'. That, in itself, generates a great sustaining power.

****

In October 2008 I was fortunate enough to take up the post of Chief Executive Officer with the Welsh Council on Alcohol and Other Drugs. This will provide me with a golden opportunity to achieve my newfound goal of becoming a 'giver' rather than a 'taker' – a role that I am determined to fill with energy and vision and, I hope, humility.

The Welsh Council on Alcohol and Other Drugs is a Registered Charity established in 1968 as a successor to the temperance movements. However, in these more modern times, it promotes 'Choice and Responsible Living' as opposed to temperance.

The word 'choice' is important because it embraces the

open-minded principles promoted at Clouds House* – from where I have drawn much inspiration.

The Council has given its unreserved support to a wide-ranging and comprehensive three-year development plan, which includes:

Promoting the establishment of a free, bilingual day-care rehabilitation centre incorporating structured programmes for anyone experiencing difficulties relating to alcohol, drugs (prescribed or illicit) or any other addiction or dependency.

In this centre, which will be located in Cardiff, it is proposed to have an all-embracing approach to addiction treatment across the spectrum, working in cooperation with all the other service providers in the area.

However, I've become more convinced than ever that detoxification is an essential step on the road to full recovery. A full recovery from addiction, to my mind, means being free from the compulsion to drink or use drugs or other substances to change the way we feel. And in order to achieve that goal, the person's compulsive behaviour has to stop. Only when that behaviour stops can we realistically begin to address all the other factors that can have such a negative effect on one's emotions, and improve the quality and meaning of life.

Early in 2008, before being appointed to my post with the Council, I had the privilege of being invited to visit The Living Room project at Stevenage in Hertfordshire. This is a day-care rehabilitation centre founded by Janis Feely MBE in May 2000 and its results showed an incredibly high success rate.

---

* *In the second year of my studies, the CATS team moved to The Manor House in Warminster and became amalgamated with the charity Action on Addiction.*

Inspired by the project in Stevenage, the Cardiff centre will be named The Living Room Cardiff / Yr Ystafell Fyw Caerdydd.

The title of this book, too, is inspired by The Living Room project. For the chronic addict, it may seem at times that there is no place to turn for comfort and support – No Room To Live. But help and hope are available if we are willing to take a chance to accept them. The Living Room Cardiff / Yr Ystafell Fyw Caerdydd will always have an open door!